S0-AJV-217

THIS MUST BE THE PLACE

THIS MUST BE THE PLACE

MEMOIRS OF MONTPARNASSE
BY JIMMIE "THE BARMAN" CHARTERS

AS TOLD TO MORRILL CODY

EDITED WITH A PREFACE BY HUGH FORD
INTRODUCTION BY ERNEST HEMINGWAY

COLLIER BOOKS • MACMILLAN
PUBLISHING COMPANY • NEW YORK
COLLIER MACMILLAN
PUBLISHERS • LONDON

Copyright © 1989 by Judith Alden Cody

Introduction copyright © 1989 by Hugh Ford
Copyright © 1937, by Lee Furman, Inc.
First published in 1934 by Herbert Joseph, Ltd., Great Britain

The photographs appearing in the photo insert are
from Hugh Ford's private collection except where indicated.

All rights reserved. No part of this book may be reproduced or
transmitted in any form or by any means, electronic or mechanical,
including photocopying, recording or by any information storage
and retrieval system, without permission in writing from the Publisher.

Collier Books
Macmillan Publishing Company
866 Third Avenue, New York, N.Y. 10022
Collier Macmillan Canada, Inc.

Library of Congress Cataloging-in-Publication Data
Charters, Jimmie, 1897–
    This must be the place : memoirs of Montparnasse / by Jimme "the
    Barman" Charters, as told to Morrill Cody; edited with a preface by
    Hugh Ford; introduction by Ernest Hemingway. — 1st Collier Books
    ed.
        p. cm.
    Includes index.
    ISBN 0-02-042381-0
    1. Charters, Jimmie, 1897– . 2. Montparnasse (Paris, France)-
-Social life and customs.   3. Paris (France)—Social life and
customs—20th century.   4. Bartenders—France—Paris—Biography.
5. Montparnasse (Paris, France)—Intellectual life.   6. Paris
(France)—Intellectual life—20th century.   I. Cody, Morrill, 1901–
    II. Ford, Hugh D., 1925– .   III. Title.
    DC752.M8C5   1989
        944'.361—dc19   89-476   CIP

Macmillan books are available at special discounts for bulk purchases
for sales promotions, premiums, fund-raising, or educational use.
For details, contact:

> Special Sales Director
> Macmillan Publishing Company
> 866 Third Avenue
> New York, N.Y. 10022

First Collier Books Edition 1989

Designed by Erich Hobbing

10 9 8 7 6 5 4 3 2 1

Printed in the United States of America

Walking ten feet or so ahead of me was Flossie, both of us on our way from the Dôme to the Dingo. As Flossie came abreast of the bar entrance, a handsome Rolls-Royce drove up to the curb and from it stepped two lavishly dressed ladies.

For a moment they hesitated. They looked at the Dingo questioningly. They peered in the windows between the curtains.

Flossie, seeing them, looked her contempt. As she passed into the bar she tossed a single phrase over her shoulder: "You bitch!"

Whereupon the lady so addressed nudged her companion anxiously. "Come on, Helen," she said. "*This must be the place!*"

CONTENTS

vii

CONTENTS

ILLUSTRATIONS BY HILAIRE HILER

FOREWORD BY HUGH FORD

Only a new arrival in Paris in the 1920s would ask, "Who is Jimmie Charters?" Long before leaving he would learn that Jimmie Charters was the most popular—and beloved—bartender in a city where years of artistic and political ferment had turned cafés and bars into celebrated landmarks. In the years following World War I, these establishments grew crowded and noisy, catering to the flocks of genuine and quasi-artists and writers and tourists who descended on Paris in search of inspiration, fame, entertainment, or nothing at all. Jimmie Charters will always be associated with the Dingo, a small bar that catered to well-off English and Americans and where, in May 1925, the now-famous meeting between F. Scott Fitzgerald and Ernest Hemingway finally took place. But whether in the Dingo, the Bar de l'Opera, the Parnasse, the Falstaff, the Hole-in-the-Wall, the Jockey, the Jungle, the Trois et As, which Charters called his "best bar," or in any of the many other colorful places where he served and where his loyal clientele followed him, Jimmie was the main attraction.

Something of a celebrity himself, Jimmie Charters knew celebrities by the dozen, beginning with Duff Twysden and Pat Guthrie, those hapless habitués of the Dingo whom Hemingway transformed into Lady Brett Ashley and Mike Campbell in *The Sun Also Rises*. And Hemingway himself seldom missed a day without dropping by for a drink and a chat with Jimmie, although, as Charters noticed, after his novel appeared Hemingway stayed away when Duff and Pat were there. To another of Jimmie's bars, the Parnasse, a rendezvous for prostitutes, came Isadora Duncan, often with the American painter Bob Chanler. Jimmie liked

Isadora because no matter how much she drank, she never lost her gaiety. Neither did the uninhibited Kiki, model and mistress to artists Soutine, Modigliani, Foujita, and Man Ray. No less restrained were other of Jimmie's favorites: the shipping heiress Nancy Cunard; Nina Hamnett, an English painter with a repertoire of bawdy songs; and Flossie Martin, a vivacious ex–chorus girl from New York whose prodigality kept her permanently popular but penniless. Jimmie's patrons were of a quieter disposition, too. Former political critic Harold Stearns, known in Paris as the "Hippique Buddha," preserved a solitary silence. So did Ezra Pound's protégé Cheever Dunning, and, unless provoked, Ford Madox Ford, Djuna Barnes, and Norman Douglas seldom created disturbances in Jimmie's bars.

No one could resist Jimmie's charm, his ingratiating manners, his boyish ("Liverpool") grin, but what impressed everybody most of all was his unerring tact. Charters seemed to sense, with sure accuracy, exactly what his patrons wanted, and he did his best to make them happy. If they liked to be addressed as "Mister," Jimmie did. If they needed a taxi to take them home after a night's drinking but had no money, Jimmie called one and paid the fare. If they wanted to talk to someone confidentially at the bar, Jimmie retired beyond earshot. When customers collapsed from too much to drink, he picked them up. When they argued and fought, as Robert McAlmon and Laurence Vail sometimes did, he gently but effectively separated them. Jimmie took pride in his ability to understand the people he served, to enter into their joys and woes. In return, he received a liberal education.

A naturally gregarious, friendly person, with an ease of manner gained from years of mixing with people, Jimmie perfected a dependable trick to bring strangers together in his bars. Rather than introduce them to one another, a liberty that would have exceeded the limits of propriety, he would subtly throw out a topic to which (he guessed, usually rightly) they would respond. What followed was often a conversation that made them friends. When Duff Twysden said of Jimmie, "He's one of us," as she did of certain characters in *The Sun Also Rises,* she meant that Charters belonged to the fraternity of "Us" because his character granted him membership. People felt his humanity "as a person rather than a servant," and respected him for it, and not because of any literary or artistic accomplishment.

When the news leaked out in the early 1930s that Jimmie Charters intended to write his memoirs, many who feared they had told him too much, or worse, "all," asked him not to mention them in any "scandalous manner." The request was unnecessary, for Jimmie had decided that, although writing an "uncensored book" would be "lots of fun," he would honor the confidentiality that customarily exists between bartenders and patrons and remain what he had always been, a gentleman. Gossip he would eschew. Besides, he admitted, setting down *all* that he had collected during ten years in Montparnasse would require at least twenty volumes, and most of the stories would be unprintable anyway. He would record only what he had seen and heard, along with what others had told him, and relate everything in a "simple and straightforward" manner.

Marcel Duchamp (in a letter to Jimmie Charters) called Montparnasse the first international colony of the arts, superior to Montmartre, Greenwich Village, or Chelsea, and even exceeding in importance the old Latin Quarter in Paris. In the latter, the essence of the arts had always been the students; in Montparnasse, artists of all countries and of all ages provided a more mature expression. Contributing to its preeminence, Duchamp further noted, were the "nonproductive characters of Montparnasse." It was an observation Jimmie echoed in his own reflections. The life in the bars, he claimed, the general habits and demeanor of a large number of their inhabitants, helped to shape the careers of those who became the period's outstanding creators. What Jimmie might have added was that a few among those who produced that unfettered atmosphere of the bars served as models for memorable fictional figures. For the portrait of the eloquent Dr. Matthew-Mighty-grain-of-salt-Dante-O'Connor in *Nightwood,* Djuna Barnes used Dan Mahoney, a former medical doctor whose rambling and sometimes obfuscating talk Barnes listened to with unabated attention at the Dingo and other bars. Robert McAlmon also depicted Mahoney in his short story "Miss Night." For the portrait of the investigator Wiltshire Tobin in her novel *Monday Night,* Kay Boyle drew on her association with Harold Stearns. Earlier, Stearns had turned up as Harvey Stone in *The Sun Also Rises.*

But with some exceptions, notably Hemingway, the habitués of the Dingo and other places were not the doers, the workers, those who had come to Paris to write or paint. More often than not, they were the ones who talked about writing and painting, drank, and talked some more. A few, like Robert McAlmon, tried to combine work and play, but without much success. Jimmie's followers formed a community of idlers who, without visible employment, appeared to live comfortably and had enough to eat and plenty to drink. How they managed was a perpetual mystery, one that they often cunningly sustained by saying they were broke. It was a trick to frustrate panhandlers, who were always in abundance. It is hardly an exaggeration to say that at some point everyone in the Quarter borrowed from everyone else. But if a person had a reputation for repaying his debts, it served to prepare people like Jimmie for a touch. That Jimmie's favors were so often repaid is as much a measure of the borrower's loyalty to him as it is of the steady flow of private funds, mostly from the United States, into Montparnasse. After the Wall Street crash in 1929, the flow stopped, and for many the idle—and ideal—life ended.

Jimmie's crowd, despite their artistic inactivity, excelled in gossip and self-revelation. They turned the bars and cafés in Montparnasse into places of excitement and spontaneity and even creativity. Paris would have been less lively without them. Unsparing of themselves and others, they occupied what the journalist Alex Small called a "glass house" in which everyone threw stones, although Montparnasse was not a particularly malicious place. It was widely assumed that everybody was interesting and therefore should contribute to the general entertainment a portrait of his character, and the more amusing it was the better. Small found the penchant for unbosoming one's more intimate secrets to relative strangers unimaginable anywhere else in the world. It seemed that everyone had come to Paris expressly to explain himself, and when he had finished talking, what one did not know about another's life, as well as his opinions on every conceivable topic, was inconsequential. Whatever rules of behavior had formerly been observed in conducting a proper conversation among men and women were completely abandoned. Such a lack of restraint gave everyone the feeling of inhabiting a unique place indeed.

Like a night at the Dingo, the book that bears Charters's name is not entirely of his making. It is a collaboration, a composition by many hands. The first to suggest the idea to Charters, according to Morrill Cody, the man who eventually wrote the book, was Jimmie's friend Hilaire Hiler, an American artist and jack-of-all-trades, who for a short time in the 1920s operated a popular club in Montparnasse called the Jockey. Hiler, who was as familiar with Montparnasse as Charters, even began "ghosting" the book before other interests forced him to stop. In 1932, Hiler persuaded Cody to assume the project. An experienced journalist who had lived in Paris longer than either Hiler or Charters, Cody retained a stenographer named Frances Robinson to take down everything Jimmie could remember about everyone he had ever known in Montparnasse. From Hiler and Ivan Opffer, a Danish-American painter and illustrator, Cody collected drawings of Jimmie and a few of his colorful clients, and from Mary Reynolds and Florence Gilliam, also longtime Paris residents, he gathered additional stories and anecdotes.

Another who urged Jimmie to write his memoirs was Ernest Hemingway. The two men became close friends in the mid-1920s when Jimmie worked at the Dingo. Hemingway was delighted to learn that Charters had been a professional boxer (flyweight) before arriving in Paris. That accomplishment as well as Jimmie's extraordinary bartending abilities and his unspoiled nature turned Hemingway into one of his staunchest admirers. Jimmie was different from that "weird lot" which, Hemingway complained, had infested Montparnasse and turned it into a detestable place.

He was a "good guy," genuine and sympathetic. He was like the model Kiki, another person Hemingway was fond of. Both were uneducated, original, and honest, and both personified a Montparnasse that was gone forever.

Perhaps their vestigial importance explains Hemingway's abiding interest in two relatively unknown personalities and, in turn, his contributions (in the form of prefaces) to their memoirs. With the possible exception of Sisley Huddleston's books, Kiki's *Memoirs* (1930) and *This Must Be the Place* (1934) are the earliest memoirs about Paris to be written during or close to the time in which the events described occurred. Soon after Cody had begun collecting material for Jimmie's book, he wrote to Hemingway in Key West and asked him to write a preface. If he liked the contents, Hemingway replied, he would do it. In November 1933, in Paris en route to Africa, Hemingway joined Cody and Charters at Sylvia Beach's bookshop, Shakespeare & Co., to look over the results of their collaboration. What he read and proclaimed "a fine job," Cody later revealed, consisted of little more than a hodgepodge of notes and anecdotes, many of them potentially libelous, requiring substantial revision and in some cases excision before publication. Much of the "unprintable material" Hemingway took to Africa, and neither Cody nor Charters ever saw it again.

Although Jimmie exclaimed that Hemingway's preface (posted from Nairobi, Kenya, in January 1934) would make him "a thousand times more proud than the whole book," it is doubtful that he perceived its implications and the author's intentions. Angered by Gertrude Stein's remarks about him in her autobiography (*The Autobiography of Alice B. Toklas*), installments of which he had read in the *Atlantic Monthly,* Hemingway had made the preface a rejoinder. It was the first public attack on his erstwhile friend. Besides calling him "yellow," Stein had accused him of being the creation of Sherwood Anderson and herself and of having learned about writing from serving as proofreader for *The Making of Americans,* her weighty saga of proliferating American families. What had inspired these spiteful remarks, Hemingway declared, was Stein's realization that sometime in the 1920s

Hemingway had become tired of seeing her and listening to her pontificating and had stopped appearing at gatherings in her salon. But not even a disloyal member of a salon, if he is considered important, as Hemingway had now discovered he was, can expect to be left out of an autobiography when including him will enhance its value. That all she had written was as false and malicious as the slander that might have come from the mouth of any girl around the Dôme or Sélect was infuriating. In contrast to the shameful conduct of this ambitious, self-made legendary woman, concluded Hemingway, Jimmie Charters not only "gave less and better advice" but he "served more and better drinks than any legendary woman every did in her salon."

While preparing this new edition of Charters's memoir for publication, I visited Morrill Cody, whom I had known for several years and with whom I coauthored *The Women of Montparnasse* (1984). Cody lived in Front Royal, Virginia, a stopping-off place for travelers leaving or joining the Skyline Drive that winds through the Blue Ridge Mountains. Nothing in Front Royal reminds one of Paris, but in his home on a quiet, shady residential street were the memorabilia of his many years in the French capital: paintings by Foujita, Man Ray, and Matisse; autographed books by his friends Virgil Thomson, Sylvia Beach, and Hemingway; letters from Franco-American compatriots; snapshots taken in the Dingo and outside the Jockey.

Cody and I often discussed a matter that has concerned many who were in Paris in the 1920s: the distortion and romanticizing of the time, the place, and the inhabitants. "What happened in Montparnasse," Cody observed, "was neither as glorious nor as notorious as it has been made out to be. How we lived and what we did have fossilized into a fanciful myth. One part of the myth presents us as a libidinous gang of immoderate drinkers and philanderers. Another part depicts us as a harmonious community of generous-minded artists congregating in cafés to discuss high art and share our latest theories. That we were neither one nor the other is a point Jimmie's book makes. And, incidentally, we were not very 'wicked' either. 'Wild' would be a more accurate word. When Jimmie and I chose 'Wicked Montparnasse' for the title of the first chapter, we were being intentionally ironic, just as Robert McAlmon was when he named his memoirs *Being Geniuses Together*. McAlmon knew there was much more affectation than real genius in Montparnasse, and Jimmie knew that a show of contrived sin, or depravity, was often mistaken for wickedness."

Morrill Cody died in 1987, and even with his testament to Jimmie Charters, Paris in the 1920s will always stimulate the fancy of those who write about it. It stimulated Fitzgerald when he renamed it "Babylon," and Hemingway when he called it "A moveable feast," and Henry Miller, a little later, when he transformed it into a "Tropic of Cancer." Interpretations will always elevate the romantic over the real, and memory, for those who were there, may do the same. Certainly it should be said, as Hemingway already has, that the memory of each person who has lived in Paris will differ from that of any other. What Jimmie Charters remembered and deigned to set down about his famous, infamous, or now-forgotten friends and customers and about the place where they played and worked is an engaging and realistic picture of Paris as it was for a few timeless years between world wars.

Once a woman has opened a salon it is certain that she will write her memoirs. If you go to the salon you will be in the memoirs; that is, you will be if your name ever becomes known enough so that its use, or abuse, will help the sale of the woman's book. Even if your name means nothing to those strange folk who pay cash for literary reminiscences (I understand they have been banded into clubs or guilds, perhaps for their own protection) you will still have your place in the memoirs if you will devote yourself loyally enough and long enough to serving the cause of the woman and of her salon, and quite too often, of her art. Such women usually write but they have been known to practice sculpture and to paint as well. But if you are mentioned only for loyalty to the establishment and for services rendered you must not expect a very lengthy citation.

The best way to achieve an exhaustive mention (outside of having the salon woman purchase your sculpture, your paintings, your wash drawings, or perhaps your embroidered diapers, if embroidering is your art, while these objects are still very cheap and continue to hold them after they become expensive so that mention of them would be calculated to increase their value) is to have the woman be fond of you and then get over it. The reasons for the getting over it may be many: You may be no longer so young; you may lose your teeth, your hair, your disposition, your money, your shoes, your shirts may not come back from the laundry; anything, in fact. Or you may get very tired of seeing the woman or of hearing her talk. It may be that the getting over it is induced by domestic compulsion, or by the changes of the seasons, or it may be anything you say, but the memoir writer will usually prove that a lady's brain may still be between her thighs—but let us not make jokes about thighs—and will treat you in her memoirs exactly as any girl around the Dôme or the Sélect would; imputing you this, denying you that and only withholding the Billingsgate because it would fit illy in the pantheon of her own glory that every self-made legendary woman hopes to erect with her memoirs.

That is how to achieve a lengthy mention, if you want one. But you must start young. Literary ladies like them young or famous; and not too famous and famous in some other line. Literary salon women do not like Mr. James Joyce for instance. They would be happier if there had not been any Mr. James Joyce. However, if you go to the salon you must expect to be in the memoirs.

Now a saloon, or bar, is different. You should expect to be able to go into a saloon or bar and pay for your drinks without appearing in the bartenders' memoirs and I was shocked and grieved to hear that Jimmie Charters was writing his. It is only a step from abolishing the right of sanctuary in the Republic of San Marino to permitting bartenders to write their memoirs and surely Jimmy served more and better drinks than any legendary woman ever did in her salon, certainly Jimmy gave less and better advice. I can hear him saying "You should go home, sir. Shall I get a taxi?" and if he wants to write his memoirs, it is only one more step in the decline of Western civilization. Besides I am very fond of Jimmy. He was always charming and he was and is an excellent barman. Like everyone else in Montparnasse, the most interesting part of his life was before he crossed to the Left Bank of the Seine, but, like almost everyone else there, he did not realize that. If he writes his memoirs I hope he gets that early part in and I wish him luck with all of it. If his book has only one-half of his charm, one-quarter of his knowledge, and one-quarter of his experience it should still be a fairly intoxicating volume. I wish it were not about Montparnasse because that is a dismal place. But Jimmy could make it very cheerful when he was behind the bar. Here's luck to him putting it in a book!

ERNEST HEMINGWAY

WICKED MONTPARNASSE

A broad boulevard lined on either side with shops, restaurants, cafés, and apartment houses, a public bath or two, a church set back from the street, at one end a railway station, at the other an impressive corridor of trees leading into the delightful Luxembourg Gardens—that is the Boulevard du Montparnasse whose fame has spread over the entire world. On the map you will see that Montparnasse is well removed from the Latin Quarter where Trilby lived, though the two quarters are often confused. The exodus of the painters and sculptors from the Latin Quarter started well before the war, so that by 1919 there was quite a colony of artists whose life centered on the Café de la Rotonde, then the only drinking place of importance in the neighborhood. By 1921 English and American artists had begun to seek studios in this new "home of the gods and the poets." By 1925 thousands upon thousands were pouring into Montparnasse every year, from every country in the world, many of them mere curiosity seekers, others bent on a few months of "escape" from the restraints of home environment, few of them serious artists.

In 1925 Montparnasse reached its pinnacle of success, the point where artists, tourists, and madmen mixed in equal parts in a gay abandon to the pleasures of the moment. But then the tide began to turn. The number of tourists and onlookers became disproportionately high. Too much advertising had turned the spontaneity of "la vie de bohème" into a huge commercial success. The old-timers and the serious artists began to move out, not to any one quarter, but to scattered and often outlying districts. It was the beginning of the end, though the cafés continued to flourish mightily until the depression swept most of the Americans and English—the biggest spenders, of course—back to their native lands.

But it is the 1923–1925 period I want to write about, when some of the most brilliant people in the world were my customers on the other side of the bar. The Dôme, across the street from the Rotonde, had by that time become the center around which everyone gravitated. This came about because, back in those moralistic days, a "lady" did not smoke in public. Neither did she appear on the street without a hat. But one spring morning the manager of the Rotonde looked out on the *terrasse,* or sidewalk section, of his establishment to discover a young American girl sitting there quite hatless and smoking a cigarette with a jaunty air. Her hatlessness he might have overlooked, but the smoking—No! He immediately descended on her and explained that if she wished to smoke, she must move inside.

"But why?" she asked. "The sun is lovely. I am not causing any trouble. I prefer to stay here."

Soon a crowd collected. The onlookers took sides. Several English and Americans loudly championed the girl. Finally the girl rose to her feet and said that if she could not smoke on the terrace she would leave. And leave she did, taking with her the entire Anglo-American colony!

But she didn't move far. Across the street was the Dôme, which up to that time had been a small bistro for working men, housing on the inside one of those rough green boxes which the French so flatteringly call a billiard table. Accompanied now by quite a crowd, the young lady asked the manager of the Dôme if she might sit on the terrace *without* a hat and *with* a cigarette. He immediately consented, and from that time forth the Dôme grew to international fame and became the symbol for all Montparnasse life.

Of course, the Rotonde retained a goodly clientele, for there was room for both cafés and a lot more besides, but it was largely filled with Russians, Germans, and visitors from the Balkan States. Later it became a communist center and was raided a couple of times by the police. Today it is closed entirely. And the funny part is that the Rotonde really had a much better location than the Dôme, because it received the pleasantly warm morning sun, while the only the hot afternoon sun. Many a morning I have been on the Dôme terrace with a group of friends, all of us wishing we could be sitting in the bright sunlight that bathed the almost empty terrace across the street, but all of us equally unwilling to break the tradition that English and Americans did not patronize the Rotonde!

The Dôme soon expanded from a bistro to a big, garish café with rows and rows of tables inside and out. Most of the day it was well filled, but toward evening it was almost impossible to find a seat unless you knew the waiter or saw friends who had already cornered a table. Around you people milled in a slow-moving stream. They were a motley crowd—tall, raw-boned Swedes, sleek Russians and Spaniards, noisy Americans, self-conscious English, anxious or portly French, all intent on their own affairs or minutely searching the crowd for a friend or sucker. Women dressed in the height of fashion rubbed elbows with shabby models or gaudy prostitutes; a rotund gentleman with flowing artist tie caused a stir among the young painters who flocked to exhibit acquaintance with one who had "arrived"; a beggar woman clutching a dirty brat held out a grubby hat; two young bloods started a fistfight until a waiter pushed them into the street and they walked off arguing; at the next table a cluster of tourists gaped and pointed.

But, though the Dôme was the most important café and the one best known to the world at large, it was far from the only one. In the half mile which stretches from the Montparnasse station to the Place de l'Observatoire, there were more than thirty establishments where, for a modest price, one could slake his thirst. In the side streets there were innumerable others. Each had a character of its own. L'Avenue, for instance, was very French, old-fashioned, dignified, while at the other end of the Boulevard du Montparnasse, the Closerie des Lilas maintained all the traditions of the old Latin Quarter. Some were big, some very small, but all of them were well patronized, for from the ends of the earth thousands upon thousands came to Montparnasse to drink to the discovery of newfound ideas in art, unaccustomed freedom, new loves, or escape from the commonplace. A few, like the two overpainted girls down in front, or the con man in the corner, were seeking a living.

Physically Montparnasse was little more than a gray and dull street holding a broken double row of cafés, but in spirit it was stronger than home or religion, the ultimate of the social reaction to the war. Whoever had troubles with his parents or his wife, whoever was bored with the conventions of stability, begged or borrowed the money to come to Montparnasse, led on by a promise of complete escape. Never has there been such an international gathering of more or less brainy excitement seekers. And excitement they found! But it was excitement with a purpose. It was organized rebellion against all in the world that is narrow and confining.

Some have pretended that Montparnasse was a band of drunks, perverts, degenerates steeped in immorality. Others show it as a sanctimonious or crudely sensational haven of intellectuals. It was neither and it was both. All kinds were for once woven into a close community determined to enjoy the things they had always wanted. They learned from each other the subtleties and cruelties of life. Businessmen became artists, pillars of the church became degenerates, drunkards became poetic. Men and women argued over new theories of life and then proceeded to try them out. There was no limit to this freedom.

The Dôme, as I have said, was the focal point for the English and Americans. In the normal course of events you went there in the morning, or whenever you got up, for a breakfast of croissants and coffee, to read the morning paper, and to rehash with your friends the events of the night before. That finished, you wandered off to your occupation of the day. If you were an artist you might attend classes at one of the art academies nearby; if a writer, you returned to your apartment, or with a friend or two you might go off on some excursion to other parts of Paris, to a museum or the races, to your bank for mail, or to luncheon with a Right-Banker on the Champs Élysées. But by afternoon, you would be back again on the terrace of the Dôme drinking your aperitif, that stimulating forerunner of the night to come.

For dinner you would collect your friends and depart to some "little" restaurant where they served some specialty of which you or they were particularly fond. This restaurant might be nearby, but more than likely it was in another quarter. Dinner would last for a couple of hours, but nine or ten o'clock would almost surely see you back on the Dôme terrace again!

There you would meet a new set of friends, your original party would break up and a new one form. Suddenly someone would say, "Let's go round to the Dingo," or it might be the Falstaff or the Trois et As or the Jockey. Those were a few of the smaller, more intimate bars where the management catered exclusively to foreigners and the few internationally minded French. Prices were high in such places, but that only served to keep out the riffraff. Probably you had your favorite bar where you knew the waiter, owner, and barman by their first names, and where you knew practically every client, at least by sight. Here you settled down to serious drinking because, to your dismay, you found that there were several of your friends who were already well ahead of you.

These smaller bars really took the place of the American living room. No one ever entertained at home, first because French housing laws do not permit *any* noise after ten o'clock, and secondly because it was so much more economical to meet your friends in a bar where each paid for his own drink. In this manner there was no bother of giving invitations or keeping dates. Knowing, as most Quarterites did, several hundred other Montparnassians, you were certain to encounter at least three or four congenial souls no matter what bar you visited!

And so, night after night, these smaller bars would be packed to the moldings with groups of Anglo-Saxons of all kinds. For hours they would sit there telling stories, discussing art and literature, flirting, or sometimes just sitting. Around one o'clock some would depart for Montmartre and the nightclubs where American-negro orchestras provided excellent dancing; a few of the more hard-working would go home; but most of them stayed right on until closing time at three o'clock. Finally, forced out by the management, many would simply move over to the Dôme again, which stayed open all night. There, between four and five, they would meet the stragglers returning from the Montmartre "dancings" and there would be a final nightcap all around preparatory to going home.

Of course not everyone lived up to such a schedule every night, though a few of them tried. For most, however, it was a matter of two or three times a week.

It was in such an atmosphere that I found myself in 1924 as assistant barman at the Dingo. I had previously been working on the Right Bank and I had visited many of the Montparnasse establishments during 1923, especially the Jockey, which I will describe in a later chapter. It was because I was fascinated by the camaraderie of Montparnasse that I was so anxious to work there.

At that time I was a young English boy, undersized, shy, awed, but anxious to please. My experience behind the bar was slight and never before one of personal friendship with the clients. All I could offer was what the writer Sam Putnam calls my "Liverpool grin," a perpetual expression of my desire to be sympathetic. I still have the Liverpool grin. It is my principal stock-in-trade.

It is hard for me to describe myself. I was thin, then, and now I am fat. I am short but strong, from my years in professional boxing. I do not think I am like the usual barman; I even pride myself on my difference. Almost anyone can learn to mix drinks accurately and fast. That is the least of it. I have always believed success behind the bar comes from an ability to understand the man or woman I am serving, to enter into his joys or woes, make him feel the need of me as a person rather than a servant. And yet—and this is so important—to keep my place. It is sometimes hard to draw the line. There are men I have addressed as "Mister" for ten years, and probably will for another ten years, whom I know better than their best friends. Still they know, and I know, that we are close personal friends. I have been entertained by them; I have sometimes been drunk with them; they have told me their most intimate secrets; but I am still a barman to them.

This business of taking an occasional but ever-recurring part in the lives of others has a fascination for me. I took my Montparnasse seriously. I think I brought happiness to many people by being tactful, by keeping them from doing things they might regret, by building friendships among congenial souls. Any barman can do this, though most won't bother. I bothered only because I found it a highly fascinating occupation.

I have a letter here from Sam Putnam and perhaps it will tell, better than I can tell, about me:

"There is something about Montparnasse madness that is a blinding white clarity. I have experienced such a sensation more than once as I stood up at Jimmie's bar in the old rue du Montparnasse. The alcoholic cloud would suddenly lift; and there, lo and behold, was Jimmie standing behind the bar as usual with that Liverpool grin on his face and saying, 'What'll you have?'—it was always 'What'll you have?' with Jimmie. For myself, I usually, like Mr. Hemingway's children, took another one. It's the best thing to take, always, bullfight or no bullfight. I would be standing there, and I would suddenly see that cloud lift, and I would glance down the bar, at the Countess or Sam, her escort, or Wambly Bald, or Hilaire Hiler, or Homer Bevans, or—God knows who—and I would be dead sober, and there was Jimmie saying, 'What'll you have?'

"I can see Jimmie yet, reaching across the bar, gentle like, to put an obstreperous customer to sleep—gently, oh, so gently—then, one hand on the bar and he's across, picking the guy up, dusting him off, and sending him home in a taxi—*and* paying his fare! That was Jimmie. I often wondered how he made any money.

"But those days are gone forever now. I know they are for me. The other day I ran into Homer Bevans in New York and we went into Thompson's and drowned our memoirs in buttermilk. Homer tried to tell me how better it all was. I wouldn't listen. Montparnasse may be the explanation of my liver, but I wouldn't have missed it for all that. Livers be damned! I've got something to tell my great-grandchildren about, and Jimmie to them will be a mythical character—which is exactly what he is."

And so I have presumed to write a book on Montparnasse—not without many misgivings—because I have been at the very fountain of this postwar freedom. I have seen it start and finish from the only all-observing position—across the bar. I am without formal education. I do not understand the principles of life, though I have spent hundreds of hours listening to others discussing them. But into this book I can put what I have seen and remembered, and leave it to the critics to add the theories.

I had never been in a madhouse before I went to Montparnasse. I had never seen people drink to get drunk; never seen artists, writers, nobles, American sailors, and doubtful women mingle on equal terms without reserve.

Perhaps my ignorance was an advantage. Looking back over those years in the heyday of the quarter, I realize how naive I was about it all. I was unimpressed by the great names because most of them were unknown to me. What I can tell of Montparnasse is a record of the people who stand out in my mind as personalities, both likeable and not so likeable. I have seen them in their unguarded moments and appreciated them for their worth of character rather than their achievements in art or literature.

In this book I want to tell of the real Montparnasse, the life in the bars which, I think, was the starting point of many a career. The few that have made a name for themselves are a result of the general habits and life of a large number.

I will never forget my first impressions of the Dingo. The crowd would start to drift in any time after noon, sad individuals with hangovers, or small and quite sober groups of earnest men and women discussing art, which seemed to be an inexhaustible subject. I didn't understand much about the art but I could see my clients were very serious about it and I tried to be sympathetic. The hangovers took pick-me-ups and the others sipped their drinks slowly, but by five o'clock the crowd was in full swing. And such an uproar! Excited women, amorous couples, jittering fairies, gay dogs, overserious young men expounding theories, and a few quiet, observing souls who took it all in and appreciated it. The intoxication was in the drinks, but also in the spirit of freedom from all the conventions and ties that bound these people at home.

During dinner there was a lull, but soon things were going again, to last right through to closing time. During the evening I was called upon not only to mix many drinks but also to settle fights, listen to intimate confidences, prevent jealousies, arrange parties, and crack jokes. I never worked so hard in all my life, enjoying every minute of it!

Our clients in the Dingo were largely English and Americans with plenty of money to spend, and parties often went on for three days without sleep or rest. "Buy a drink for the bar" was a favorite cry in those days, which meant that someone offered a drink to every person standing at the bar, sometimes twenty or thirty of them. I don't remember that anyone ever refused. Then the client would hand me a large note. "Keep the change," he would say, which sometimes amounted to as much as the bill! Those were prosperous days for me, though unfortunately I spent my money as fast as I earned it. France was in an inflation period and brand-new notes were being given out at the banks. Sometimes two or even three hundred-franc notes would stick together and neither the client nor I would notice it at the time. Later, when I counted my money, I would find myself richer by several hundred francs. So anxious were the people to spend they would try to pay me several times for the same drinks, or, on the spur of the moment, pay for someone else's bills for no good reason. Many of the girls who always hang around bars covered all their bills for food and drink by this method.

I used to sell things over the bar, too, to make a little money. Once I bought a dog for two hundred francs and sold him half an hour later to an American for two thousand. He bought him on my promise that he would never grow any bigger. I gave the promise knowing nothing about it, and the man took him to America.

Years later he told me the dog grew to twice the size, but he loved him anyway!

Another source of revenue for me in those days was the exchange. Someone with a ten-pound note would want it changed into francs. I would not have enough spare money to give him the full value but would offer him half, the rest to be collected the next day. Many clients never came back for the other half of their money.

Tips, too, were very generous. Count Karolyi, the former prime minister of Hungary, who was a very good client of mine, always gave me as a tip more than the total of the bill. For instance, if he had a five-franc drink he would give me twelve francs. Once, from another client, I had a tip of a thousand francs on a bill which had run over a period. I guess I'll never see those days again! Today a barman feels pleased to get a five-franc tip!

Of course we had some who were not so generous and others who ran out of money entirely. I used to have a great collection of watches and pins which had been left with me as security and which were never called for. We let some of the clients run up bills, too, and many of them were never paid. I am told the unpaid bills over a nine-year period in the Dingo totaled half a million francs, despite efforts at care. In another chapter I will tell more about this business of credit.

But please do not get the impression Montparnassians were just a band of drunks. To give such an idea would be entirely false. Drinking was incidental—a very important incidental, if you like—to discussion, art, "the study of human nature," lovemaking, and having a good time generally, or perhaps having a bad time generally for those who enjoyed their miseries in big gulps. The Quarter in those days was a theater on whose stage a hundred dramas were constantly being played, tangles of love, intrigue, suicide, ambition, greed, and high intellectualism. If this book seems disjointed in spots and jumps from a great poet to a visiting drunk from Wichita, it is because the life of the Quarter was just that mixture. People did not separate into class or intellectual groups. A typical bar full would be a coming painter, a prostitute, a well-known writer, a society woman, an habitual dope addict, a wealthy businessman, a model, and so on, all talking together, all friends without class consciousness, all learning from each other, all professing an interest in Art with a big A.

During an evening with such a crowd I would listen to details of a recent prizefight, details of how a young man should treat a girl in bed, details of a scheme for a transatlantic airmail route, details of a suicide—there were always plenty of details! I can't put them all in this book—the publishers tell me—and keep out of jail, but I'll put in as many as I can.

THE ART OF BARTENDING

You may smile, but there is a real art in bartending, and all good barmen must know it. Diplomacy is a first requisite, without which a man can never be a success in anything but a very formal bar. Mike, the Dingo's first barman, had it naturally. Louis Smith, who followed him, didn't, though he was a success in formal English or French bars where the client only orders and the barman only serves.

And then there are all the little tricks that the barman knows to keep his customers satisfied, little things to make the customer feel that the barman is a "good buy," as the Americans say. It was only after I left the Dingo that I realized that a barman is really more important, in many cases, than the bar itself.

First, there must be no squabbling over bills. The client must pay what he thinks he should pay, rather than have a fuss. I have seen a man sit at the bar, drink five brandies, and swear he had only four, even with the fifth check lying right in front of him. If he protests I put the check aside and either give it to him another day or pay it myself. I learned from the Americans that it always pays me to keep the customer satisfied. In practically all cases the customer thinks he is right. He does not want to cheat me. And many times he will come back later to admit he was wrong. I have never had a row over a bill and I never will.

Of course, real ladies and gentlemen won't argue over a bill. They pay and never come again. There are fewer and fewer of this type, however. Sometimes such a person will question the bill by saying "Are you sure that's right, James?" Then I know that something is wrong.

There is nothing like a "drink on the house" to make the client feel good. If I were running my own bar I would give each client a free drink for every two or three he buys. Unfortunately, many of the owners for whom I have worked have not understood this principle. They have always figured that I was putting the money for the extra drink into my own pocket. No argument would convince them to the contrary. It seems just madness, to French people, especially, to give the client something for nothing! It is a kind of madness that pays. Given a free drink, the customer always buys another or even two. He feels obligated. And he comes back the next day.

I have always tried to study my clients, to know their likes and dislikes, to keep them interested in me and in each other. A bar is a club where the members must not clash, for it is so easy to resign from a bar.

Of my clients in Montparnasse some seventy percent were Americans, about twenty percent English, and the rest a mixture of French, Italians, South Americans, and Swedes. The English and Americans always mixed well enough, but the other groups had to be kept apart, not only from the Anglo-Saxons, but from each other, if fights were to be avoided. I usually tried to steer the "odd lots" to a table, while the Anglo-Saxons thronged the bar itself.

Fights in a bar are to be avoided at all costs, of course. I can usually "smell" a fight coming on, and then I do everything to prevent it. I try to divert the combatants by telling them jokes, or by giving them drinks on the house. Usually the free drink works. In the pleasure of receiving it they forget their quarrel and drink to each other, or both drink to me, or in some way forget to be angry. In the Dingo days I had as many as sixty to eighty American sailors, or "gobs" as they were called, in the bar at one time, and if there is anyone in the world who likes a fight, it is an American sailor! Most men like to fight once in a while, but sailors do it for daily exercise.

Yet, in all my years in Montparnasse, I don't think there were ever more than two real fights. Either I quieted the combatants or put them out of the bar. If there was no other way, I would take the worst one to a bistro and park him there with a drink and a prayer that he would not come back to my bar. I don't remember ever having had to actually throw a man or woman out of the bar, though many times I have had to jump between two men who were about to slug each other.

Fights between two women are far harder to handle than among men. When I see one of these coming on I first remove all the loose objects from the bar, such as ashtrays, glasses, bottles, and plates. If things begin to get rough I threaten to call the police, for women are far more afraid of the cops than are men.

Most fights between women are caused by jealousy over a man. Very often, in Montparnasse, they were between French and Anglo-Saxons, for the former did not understand the free and easy, though harmless, ways of our girls.

Jealousy implies love, and love was a very common article in Montparnasse. I cannot begin to count the number of times I have been involved in other people's love affairs, asked to slip notes back and forth, give stronger drinks to a certain person so he or she would become more amorous, or lie to a husband or wife to ward off suspicion. I remember a married couple—Americans—who were always playing a game with each other, while I stood in the dangerous in-between ground. The wife would come in asking for her husband.

"I haven't seen him," I would reply. She would then sit down to wait, but a half hour later would depart with another man.

"Don't tell my husband you saw me," she would say in leaving. Ten minutes later the husband would arrive.

"Have you seen my wife, Jimmie?"

"No, sir, she hasn't been in." I was fortunate on such occasions if some other client didn't pipe up and say "Why Jimmie! You know she was just in here!" If not, the husband would sit down and eventually he too would depart with some chance acquaintance of the opposite sex.

"Don't tell my wife you saw me, Jimmie," he would warn in leaving.

"No, sir, I'll remember." Then sometime later the wife would return and the comedy start all over again. It kept me busy remembering whom I'd seen and whom I hadn't!

Of course people make all kinds of dates in a bar which are forgotten the next morning. Many times I have seen a man or woman make a half dozen dates for the following afternoon in my bar, and then when the time arrived not a soul would show up.

When a man or a woman comes into the bar I must size him up quickly to see if he wants to be alone or is really looking for companionship. Most people won't admit they are lonely, especially the overreserved English people who nevertheless welcome conversation with someone else. As I am serving them they will talk to me because they know me. When I have two such persons in the bar I usually manage to stand between them. First I talk to one and then I talk to the other, always trying to make them laugh at the same time. Soon they are talking to each other and I go away.

I have started many a romance in this way. Victor Pattou, the Adonis of the Quarter, met his wife Sue in this manner, and a year later he brought a tiny baby into the bar, saying, "Look what you caused, Jimmie!"

I always encourage people to talk together at a bar if they show any inclination whatsoever, for it means I will sell more drinks. But I learned long ago that people must never be introduced to each other. They may talk with pleasure, but they always resent a barman's making a formal presentation. Clients expect a barman to smile, be jovial and gay, but stay strictly within his realm. Even Americans, who are more democratic, will not stand any freshness from the barman.

There were many "lonely hearts" in the Montparnasse bars, especially women who craved the society of the male sex. Many of these women belonged to the "alimony gang," as we called them, women who came to Montparnasse after a divorce in England or

America. Once there and established in an apartment, they looked around for company, only to find that the women in Montparnasse numbered two or three for every man. Yet there were some men available, and the women came to the bars to find them.

Sometimes—a surprising number of times—these women made passes at me or at the waiters, probably out of sheer desperation. But I always steer clear of such entanglements. Very often a client—especially a woman—with whom I have been out on a party thinks she owns the place from that time on, expects free drinks, and generally makes a nuisance of herself.

So my system was to find a mate for the lonely hearts, and there was usually some man around to fall in with this scheme, whether he knew it or not. I would get her talking with the man just before closing time. When the bar finally closed he usually suggested that she go with him to the Dôme or some other café that stayed open later. But having once made up her mind, she still had her eye on me.

"I'll go," she would say, "if Jimmie comes too!"

Of course I would go along. I would buy them a drink at the café and then excuse myself, saying that I must see someone but that I'd be right back. If the girl asked me next day why I did not return I mumbled something about having been involved in a business deal.

Women have been my big problem. I suppose every man has the same problem, but not in such big doses, for almost three-quarters of my Paris clients were women. Women can hold more liquor than men, but when they get a little squiffed they almost always make themselves much more conspicuous. The homelier they are, the more they want to show off. They will stop at nothing. Very often a woman will take offense at some imaginary insult in order to attract the attention of some man present, hoping that he will rise to her defense. He often does, not knowing it is just a little game she is playing. Men do this, too, to attract women, though less often.

Why must women be so noisy when they are tight? Other

people don't like to see a woman tight, though they don't mind a man. Men drunks may be very humorous and good-natured, while women so often become complete nuisances. In particular, deliver me from the female practical joker, the woman who thinks it is humorous to pour a gin fizz down the back of another! I have had several like that.

And then there are the exhibitionists! One out of every ten women seems to be an exhibitionist with a passion for getting undressed in public. Or they try to imitate their idea of a French *poule, à la Vie Parisienne,* by cocking their legs up over their heads. I had one client, an English girl, who had a dressing gown that looked just like a street dress. She would sit at the bar and after a few drinks would pull it wide open, leaving herself stark naked underneath.

"Oh Jimmie," she would say, "I am so careless. I forgot to get dressed!" I cannot count the times I have had to wrap that dress around her and tie it securely.

You see it isn't so easy, being a bartender. You have to be prepared for all kinds of emergencies.

Liquor always has one of three effects on people. Upon a few it brings a deep depression, because, I suppose, there is some sorrow there already. On the normal person, though, the effect is either to make him amorous or belligerent, and he or she can jump from one state to the other without difficulty. If a man or woman seems to be in a fighting mood, I try to find him or her a mate, and all is peace. Then of course the two of them may become *so* amorous—but that is another story.

Other problems at a bar are the pests, the men who drink other persons' drinks, for instance. I had one man who would come in, drink every glass of beer in the room, and walk out before anyone could stop him. We finally had to turn the police on him. In France many out-and-out beggars came to the bar too, and they had to be handled carefully. We could not let them annoy our customers, yet we could not throw them out rudely for fear of annoying any French who might be in the room. Quite often a

Frenchman would call a beggar back and give him something just to annoy the Anglo-Saxons. Thus encouraged, the beggar would start on a tour of the room. Usually I gave him a franc or two on the understanding that he would not beg from the clients. The beggars came to understand that we were a bit afraid of them, and they took advantage of it, coming back again and again.

Another class we watched for were the French workingmen who thought ours was just an ordinary bistro. They would come in asking for a glass of red wine. Very often these people were peasants from the country, unused to Paris ways. So I always told them the price first, because if they found it out afterward, they never paid. Personally, I liked to get them out of the bar as fast as possible, for I never knew just what might happen, though often they were jovial old duffers who thought it was quite exciting to be with such well-dressed foreigners. Sometimes they had quite a bit of money and wanted to buy drinks for the whole crowd.

At other times, they were more difficult. Seeing women alone at a bar, they thought they must be *poules* placed there for their amusement. I hurriedly explained that "Madame is waiting for her husband," but that did not always quiet them. "*Ou sont les poupées?*" (Where are the dolls?) they demanded insistently. By law we could refuse to serve no one in a public bar, and so great tact had to be used.

The barman has so many problems, I could fill a book with them. Credit is one of the major ones and there is no way to avoid it. I can't ask a man to pay before he has been served; and then if he tells me he left his pocketbook at home, I can't call him a liar! I may or may not be paid. Many well-meaning people forget they owe me money and go off to another country or are called home suddenly without settling up. Of course such cases usually represent small bills, but they add up nonetheless.

For you must understand that it is usually the bartender himself who takes the credit, and it is he who pays the owner, whether the client pays or not. Sometimes the house takes the credit direct, as in two of my bars in Montparnasse, but this is not usual.

The most difficult for me are the old clients who, for one reason or another, go broke, but are ashamed to drop out of the bar life. In fact they feel the need of liquor all the more. They never tell me they are broke, but talk of the check that will arrive in a day or so.

"Jimmie," they will say, "I can't understand it, but my check hasn't come yet. I am afraid I'll have to run up a little bill on you until it does." What can I say? They are old clients; they have always paid before. Maybe the check does come, and maybe it doesn't. One day they go home and I am out a goodly sum. Then, too, if one of them gets into me for a goodly sum, I can't stop his credit for fear he will be angry, walk out, and everything will be gone. I tell you the life of a barman is a tough one!

Of course I try to differentiate the payers from the cheats, and, through a costly experience, I have learned a bit about it. However, it is dangerous to offend even the cheat, for he may take business away from the bar. I have lost much money through being afraid of offending people.

I stay away from the man or woman who talks too much about the money he has, or from anyone who seems to be preoccupied with money questions. When I hear a man say, "Well, Jimmie, I've never asked you for credit, have I?" I'm warned right then. I give him a few drinks and then stop all credit. Some of these credit seekers have talked my hair off in an effort to run up "just a little bill."

The professional credit seekers, of whom there are not many, use the same system over and over. It is simple. A man comes in, perhaps with friends, orders several rounds of drinks, pays for them with a generous tip, and returns the next day with other friends, still spending money easily. The third or fourth day he may run up a small bill, but the next afternoon he will be there to pay it. A little later he will leave a larger bill, which again he pays promptly the next day. But in the end he will run up considerable credit and walk out on me, never to return. Under this system a man can pay an average of about half-rate for his drinks, moving from bar to bar every few weeks. Even so it seems hardly worth it.

One of the great difficulties about bar credit in France was the law which says that a man cannot be sued for a bar bill involving *only* drinks. To be collectable, the bill must include some items of food, if only sandwiches. It is pretty hard to prove that a client in a bar consumed food with his drinks unless he voluntarily signs an acknowledgment of the debt. The law is designed to protect a man from being charged with drinks he did not have on the excuse that he was drunk and could not remember.

About ten percent of the receipts of my Paris bars represented credit, and fully half of that was never paid. As the bartender was usually paid a small salary (around a thousand francs, or forty to sixty dollars a month) plus five percent of the gross receipts, his loss from bad credit and his profit from the business broke about even. Of course we got our tips in addition, as well as food and some drinks.

The English are much the cleverest at getting credit, and I have lost more to them than to Americans. The Englishman has a slightly superior way with him that is hard to refuse, and he always has better excuses. The Americans are often clumsy and embarrassed, though there have been notable exceptions.

And women have been worse for me than men. I suppose I do not understand them so well, nor see through their excuses. It is so easy for a woman to "forget to pay." She doesn't mean to be dishonest, really. The only advantage in giving credit to a woman is that she charges only her own drinks, while a man on credit often treats the bar! Both try to borrow money from me, especially the women. "I must take a taxi home," she will say, but very often the money is used in another bar after mine closes.

Most barmen have had heavy losses with bad checks, but I have been lucky that way. In my experience I have had but three rubber checks, thanks to a few wise principles I learned early. I never accept a check on a bank in a foreign country; I never accept a check of a third person; and I size up my client to see whether it is worth his while to give me a bad check for a small sum. To issue a check without sufficient funds in the bank is a serious offense in

France, and in payment of a credit bill I took a check eagerly, for that was collectable where the bill might not be.

Frank at the Ritz and Zelli in his place in Montmartre have been real gambling bankers, taking all kinds of checks, many of which were returned. However, these two men have gambled on the goodwill thus gained to make profit anyway. I have never had enough money to do that. Zelli had whole drawers full of bad checks, mostly on English and American banks, when his place was at its height.

In general, give me the artist customer in preference to the tourist. The artist may become a regular client; he usually pays well; and he is generous with his tips.

A barman makes his real profit from the tips, which, in the old days, were very handsome. Men tip better than women, though a woman will often urge her escort to tip more than he intends; and Americans tip better than English.

The English have a curious way of tipping which I did not understand for a long time. An Englishman will order his drink and then say, "Have a drink," or "Have you got your drink?" which is to tell me that I am to take the price of a drink out of his money, whether I actually drink it or not. Of course it puts the barman on a friendly level with his client. At first, not understanding this system, I lost much money through ignorance, but later I caught on. I used to keep two or three drinks ready under the bar. One would be angostura bitters and plain water with ice, which looks just like whisky or brandy; another, black currant cordial in plain water, which looks like port; another, plain water with just a dash of bitters, which looks like "gin and it." Then when someone asked me if I "had mine" I would raise the appropriate glass from under the bar, for I believe in always drinking what the client drinks!

Another English way of tipping is to ask the barman to have a package of cigarettes or a cigar, the price of which he is to take out of the bill as a tip. The English soon dropped this method in Paris, though, and adopted the American way of leaving the tip in money. The Americans sometimes buy the barman a drink too, but they insist on seeing him drink it.

Besides our tips and salary, there are other little advantages for the barman, such as professional services offered free by doctors, lawyers, and others among his clients. Then, too, in France he obtains reduced rates at the theaters and cinemas, horse-racing tips, and even free entertainment at some of the less distinguished nightlife resorts, if you understand my meaning. When we steered clients to such places we received up to sixty percent commission, and there was always twenty-five percent commission from gambling houses, as well as free meals and drinks when we called.

The barman also gets a small commission from the French liquor people, a franc a bottle for gin, brandy, and whisky, fifty centimes to a franc for bar champagne, up to five francs for the expensive champagne in the cabarets, and twenty-five centimes a bottle on everything else. That can mount up if the bar is doing a big business. At Christmas each dealer makes the barman a present of a bottle or so of his product to take home for a little private drinking in off-hours.

It is the horse-racing tips that most barmen like best, for they seem to be inveterate gamblers. I used to be, too, but I was finally cured, though I am still not averse to taking a chance on a likely mare now and then. In some bars many of the clients are interested in racing, and then the barman must keep well informed about horses. Montparnassians were not so strong on racing though, and I think that is why I drifted out of the habit.

Barmen like to shake dice, too, and some of them are exceptionally lucky. Personally, I avoid shaking dice with a customer if I can, for either I lose, which I can't afford, or I win and the customer is annoyed. It is an unfair arrangement, anyway. If I lose, I can't force the customer to go on, but if he loses, then he continues playing until he has won again. I really prefer to lose because then there are no hard feelings.

It is funny sometimes to see the drunks when they want to shoot for their drinks. Perhaps they have run out of money and don't want to ask for credit. So they shoot dice, always cheating a little, clumsily, to make sure of winning. Of course I can say nothing.

I don't encourage dice shaking among the clients either, because when they gamble they forget to drink. Talk is a great encouragement to drinking, and there has never been any lack of that in Montparnasse.

WOMEN MADE
MONTPARNASSE

It is perhaps remarkable that the leaders and organizers of Montparnasse were largely women, from the famed Kiki to the inspiring Sylvia Beach, who, as far as I know, never entered a bar in her life, though, as she told me once, "We have always served the same clients, you, Jimmie, with drinks, I with books." The two who took the main spotlight, however, were Flossie Martin and Nina Hamnett.

Flossie, pretty and very jolly, certainly won in numbers of adherents, though it was whispered that Nina won in quality. Both girls brought to the Dingo their friends and their friends' friends until the place was jammed.

Flossie, a former chorus girl in New York, had been sent to Paris to develop her really fine voice. But she did little studying and finally stopped entirely. The fascination of the Dôme terrace in the daytime and the Dingo at night were too much for her. But Flossie was not selfish in her pleasures; quite the contrary. Many a chap, temporarily down-and-out, was helped financially by Flossie, though she had no large sums at her disposal. She was the friend of all the world, and around her was always to be found a group of English, Americans, and French, all infected by her somewhat loud but happy laughter.

The other stage director of the Dingo and Dôme was Nina Hamnett, English painter of note but remembered in Montparnasse largely for her singing of ballads like *Bollicking Bill the Sailor* (original version!), *She Was Poor But She Was Honest,* and

FLOSSIE

from a drawing by Hilaire Hiler

many others of the kind. Sometimes she would accompany herself on the guitar, or perhaps Charlie Ogle, the American photographer, would play for her. Montparnassians in those days were content to sit and listen to such songs for hours. Pizzuti's Italian restaurant across the street from the Dingo was a favorite place for the crowd to gather and listen to her.

Pizzuti, incidentally, made excellent ravioli which he offered as a sacrifice to the arts. He had a warm spot in his heart for painters and writers and felt proud that so many came to his restaurant. Later, when the restaurant failed, Pizzuti turned to tailoring and numerous Quarterites patronized him, though on the whole his ravioli was better!

I must say that Nina sang her songs extremely well, better than I have ever heard them sung since. Around her she attracted a group of admirers which included some of the intellectual lights of Montparnasse and others with resounding titles or names. In fact it became rather a joke at the Dingo, for the telephone would ring constantly for Nina and the waiter would announce in a loud voice that the Prince of something or the Count of something else wished to speak to Miss Hamnett. Nina had a great respect for titles and famous names.

But there was another side to Nina, the sailor side, I might call it. You see, the United States government in 1924 decided to help the tourist trade in France by sending there on protracted visits the U.S. S.S. *Pittsburgh,* U.S. S.S. *Memphis,* and U.S. S.S. *Detroit.* For days all Montparnasse was infested with sailors and petty officers moving in groups around Flossie and Nina. Nina actually wore a sailor uniform in Montparnasse and to Montmartre on one occasion. Both girls determined to do the honors for France and devoted themselves to this task with a thorough goodwill!

Flossie liked French policemen, too, and many of them treated her with special consideration. I remember one Fourteenth of July seeing Flossie dancing in front of the Dôme with an *agent,* the latter feeling very proud of himself to be whirling with such a pretty girl. And then passed by the brigadier of police, his superior, who frowned at him very severely. Such frowning the *agent* could not understand and began to look around for a reason. He soon found it! Flossie, in the gaiety and lightheartedness of the occasion, had pulled her skirts well above her knees, much to the delight of the crowd around them. When the poor policeman saw he was being disgraced before the very eyes of his captain, he was so embarrassed he fled up a side street and never reappeared.

I remember another Fourteenth of July when Flossie sat next to the trombonist on the platform of the bandstand before the Coupole, a large café up the street. Every time the trombonist took his instrument from his lips, Flossie kissed him! She kept this up for half an hour, though, unfortunately for him, the score called for quite a bit of tromboning. The country people standing around thought this a fine show.

Joe Zelli, the king of the nightclub district, finally offered Flossie a job. She was to be in his club every night, since her reputation and gaiety would always attract a crowd. I have been told Zelli did the biggest business of his successful career during the six months Flossie stayed at his club. And poor Flossie never earned any money for her work! Not that Zelli did not pay her a salary, but because, at the end of the month, she had drawn her money and more in providing drinks for friends who were "temporarily under financial stress."

Another colorful personage was Willie, a Dutch girl who lived in England and America. She was very popular, though she did not surround herself with a following as did Flossie and Nina. In fact Willie was just a little mysterious and was considered by some even dangerous, though there was never a gentler person in many ways. People were, at the same time, proud to know Willie.

She came from a good family in Holland and had received a thorough education. Her father had wanted her to be a boy, and to make up for her difference in sex, had tried to bring her up more as a man than a woman. He insisted, for instance, that she study chemistry, which she disliked, and abandon painting and writing, for which she had real talent.

A very amusing story surrounds Willie's life on an island off the Brittany coast, a small wooded spot on which she built a house with the aid of an American friend. Willie had been warned time and again to be careful of fire, but she continued to throw cigarette stubs around carelessly. When the brush finally caught, fire swept the entire island, leaving Willie, waist deep in the water, watching the ruin of her house and domain. To hear her describe it was a treat!

I believe they rebuilt the house, but did not stay, as the island had lost its charm without the trees and vegetation.

Willie then moved to the Dôme, where she became a local celebrity. Her distinction was greatly heightened by her very striking and sudden gestures, by her eccentric clothes, and by her black stick with ivory handle. She was never without that stick, except on rare occasions when she left me to guard it for a few hours.

Willie was a devoted friend of Jo Bennett's. Mrs. Bennett was probably the only person who came to the Quarter as a tourist and successfully made the transition into a full-fledged member of the colony. She and her Titian-haired daughter, Tanya, took a great personal interest in all the unfortunates of the Quarter, helping them financially and personally without looking down on them. Jo was a leader of freedom, and what's more, she could afford to provide it by giving large parties in Montmartre or by sending deserving but struggling artists on trips through Italy. Of course she got little thanks for it, though I don't suppose she was looking for spoken rewards.

Among the French, two women stand out, one of whom is still in the Quarter. Florianne was the first. She had been a ballet dancer before she became the queen of Montparnasse. On the strength of this fame, she opened an artists' restaurant known as Chez Florianne, which was quite successful for more than a year. She did all the cooking and serving herself.

Then a rival appeared, the model Kiki, with her extraordinary personality and vivacity, who was seen constantly at the Jockey. She was famous for her apache songs, her unusual makeup, and her acquaintance with practically everyone in Montparnasse. Kiki became so famous they made movies of her. She appeared on the

31

stage with the Japanese painter Foujita; she published her memoirs in both English and French; she even made a trip to New York. She did not like America, however, and always refused to learn any English, though she was often seen with Anglo-Saxons. She was particularly fond of American seamen. I do not suppose there is a single sailor on the U.S. S.S. *Pittsburgh* who has not toasted Kiki. Once I saw her on the Dôme terrace with thirty sailors and not another girl!

MOST WRITERS ARE DRINKERS

White wine, for some reason I do not understand, has always played a special role among artists and writers. I believe this has always been true in bohemian centers since the time of Whistler and his friends. Frank Harris insisted it was the only drink a man should take, and certainly it was the only one he indulged in. His formula for drinking was as follows:

"You should start, my boy, with white wine *nature,* but always keep an eye on your nose! When you see your nose becoming red, you should dilute the wine with Vichy, increasing the proportion of Vichy until your nose is white again, or at least only faintly pink. Then, as soon as your nose is thoroughly reinstated in its natural color, dispense with the Vichy completely until it is red again, and so on."

Once Nina Hamnett and Hilaire Hiler, the painter, took Harris to the Boeuf-sur-le-Toit, a Right Bank café, to meet Jean Cocteau, thinking that two such famous persons, who in reality are similar in character, should know each other. It would be, they thought, a memorable occasion. It was!

The Boeuf-sur-le-Toit was founded by Jean Cocteau and Moÿses, a former newspaper-and-pencil vendor with a fine personality and a genius for handling his clients. The name of the bar came from a ballet of that title produced by Cocteau. The expression is derived from the familiar tale of the man who lived in the attic of an apartment building in Paris. Here he kept a whole menagerie of birds of all kinds. Eventually his neighbors started to complain about the stench that drifted down from the attic, but he refused to get rid of his fowl. Finally the neighbors banded together and brought suit against him. Just at this time the attic dweller added a bull-calf to his zoo. The trial went along with the usual legal delays and one fine day the neighbors found themselves notorious: the court ordered the owner of the fowl and the bull-calf to dispose of them so that there might be no further annoyance to his neighbors. But alas, when the police came to enforce the order, they found that the trial had taken so long that the bull-calf had grown into a full-sized bull and that it would be impossible to get it out of the building without tearing down all the doors and passageways. Hence it remained *le boeuf sur le toit*—the bull on the roof.

But to come back to Nina and Hiler, Cocteau had been told in advance that the great Frank Harris would call at the bar that afternoon. Harris, too, had been primed. When Hamnett, Hiler, and Harris (sounds like a firm of tailors!) entered the Boeuf, Cocteau stood near the bar talking to a friend. He turned, greeted Nina and Hiler effusively, and they presented Harris.

"*Ah, oui, bonjour, monsieur,*" he said with a nod and turned his back. Harris had his hand out but it was never shaken by Cocteau. Hiler told me later that he felt terrible about it, and of course Harris was furious.

"Who is this man!" he spluttered. "Does he know that I am Frank Harris? Does he? The idea!"

This is in line with a comment that Wilde once made about Harris.

"It is fine for Mr. Harris, isn't it," said a friend to Wilde, "he is invited *everywhere*!"

"Yes," said Wilde, "Harris *is* invited everywhere—once!"

Many of the white-winers of the Quarter have been of the Sylvia Beach school. I have mentioned this lady before. It is she who still runs Shakespeare & Co., the friendly little bookshop on the rue de l'Odéon. I used to pass there almost daily when I was at the Trois et As bar nearby. She is a serious little woman with a quick, engaging smile and a sharp tongue on occasion.

She has had a big influence on the English and American writers especially, and in the old days you would find many with now-famous names sitting in the back room listening to her comments and suggestions. Many of this group were white-winers, though not by any means all of them.

Miss Beach is known, of course, as the first publisher of James Joyce's *Ulysses*. Joyce himself, who is a white-wine-totaler, I do not know, for he leads a very retired life and never visits bars, but I have known many of his friends and I have many times seen him around the Quarter. Montparnasse was very much impressed with Mr. Joyce, partly because he kept himself so aloof, I suppose. And yet he attended quiet little gatherings now and then when the intellectual foregathered to discuss whatever intellectuals discuss. (Intellectuals have always been somewhat of a mystery to me! I admit it.) He was very well liked by his friends, I believe, and it was a pleasure to see his fine sensitive face and erect figure. Lanky Myron Nutting, the American writer, was one of his particular disciples, I remember.

One of the leaders of the Beach group, with a reputation for having discovered much of the talent of Montparnasse, was Ezra Pound, the poet. He was an erratic character with strong likes and dislikes and a very keen wit. He was known, too, for his rudeness, which was colossal at times and of which he was always proud, I think. Pound finally moved to Rapallo but continued to make his existence felt in Paris by caustic letters to the local edition of the *Chicago Tribune*. When he heard of this book he sent me a postcard from Italy:

> *Best wishes—fer uplift & the 2-coat suit.*
> *Yrs.*
> *E. Pound.*

One night at the Cloche, a restaurant near the Odéon, Pound and Bob McAlmon were having dinner when an Italian who had all the earmarks of dope about him sprang at Bob and tried to knife him. I was present, and I always thought it was Pound who caught the Italian's arm and thus perhaps saved Bob's life. However, when I published this statement in an article in *Esquire,* Pound wrote to the magazine saying: "Much as I hate to contradict Jimmie

Charters, had he been at the center table instead of the one nearer the door, he would have seen that Mr. McAlmon tackled the dope peddler." Anyway, someone caught the man's arm and Bob was only slightly wounded.

Bob McAlmon was one of my best friends among the writers. He was formerly married to a wealthy English girl, member of one of the shipping families, but he gave up domestic bliss to write.

I don't know much about Bob as a writer, because I have little time for reading, but I know he's a good fighter. Perhaps our friendship sprang up because we are both small, both have an independent attitude toward others. Bob has a winning smile, and they tell me I have that, too, though I am sure it cannot be compared with his.

Bob's smile has an effect of magic that I have never seen equalled. One night a tough-looking, hard-boiled American by the name of T——— was giving a party in my bar, and during the course of the evening entertained his friends with various popular songs which he sang in a loud voice. Bob, who was at the bar with several Pernods in him, thought he could do better and launched into an aria from one of the operas. Bob, incidentally, is a good amateur singer.

But T——— did not appreciate opera, it seems. He became quite annoyed, and when Bob did not stop he started toward him with teeth clenched and fists closed. I thought there was going to be murder. "Be careful!" I whispered to Bob. But when they came face-to-face Bob simply smiled, while T——— stared at him blankly. Slowly I saw T———'s fists unclench; then I saw a slight smile come over his face; and once again Bob had charmed someone who was prepared to punch his face.

"Have a drink," said T———. "Make it a whisky and a Pernod, Jimmie." They drank and they talked and T——— was so interested in Bob he forgot all about his friends at the table until they became decidedly annoyed and threatened to leave.

But Bob has other weapons than his smile. I have seen him in the ring and I know he's a good fighter. We were in Bricktop's, a colored nightclub in Montmartre, one night when Bricktop said to him, jokingly, "Give me a kiss." Bob replied, also jokingly, with a gesture, "I will give you a punch instead!" A negro waiter, seeing the gesture, came over to hit him, but Bob was quicker and sent him sprawling. Soon the whole place was in a turmoil, Bob and myself against half a dozen colored men. Bob and I spent the night in jail, but we thought it was well worth it.

It was Ezra Pound who encouraged and finally launched George Antheil, the modern-music composer. George came from Trenton, New Jersey, where his father owned a shoe shop in which the son started his career as a clerk. But George had broader ideas and, with the boy next door, talked of the day when they would be geniuses. They found great interest in the new movements in Greenwich Village, reading avidly such magazines as *The Little Review*, published by Margaret Anderson and Jean Heap. They even corresponded with the editors and obtained encouragement from them.

With a little money saved, they set out for the Village and later George came to Paris while his friend became a professor at Columbia University. George, when he reached Montparnasse, had the good fortune to take a room over Sylvia Beach's bookshop. Through her he met many interesting people, including Pound, who therewith took a great personal interest in him. Another helpful friend was Kurt Weill, author of the modern *Opéra des Quatre Sous*. While he lived over the bookshop, George wrote his *Ballet Mécanique*, which caused so much caustic comment when produced in New York. Antheil is more appreciated in Europe, however.

George's life is very much the story of many others who have come to Montparnasse from England and America to pursue an impulse and develop an inspiration, though few of them succeed so well. That was the great excuse for Montparnasse, as the home of those with new ideas. Those ideas were developed, not only in the attics or studios, but also in the companionship and stimulation of the cafés and bars.

Another devoted friend of Miss Beach's was Ernest Hemingway with his friend Bill Bird, both of them newspapermen in those days. Hemingway was a correspondent with the *Toronto Daily Star,* a newspaper which paid him very little. In his spare time he was writing short stories, but they were not acceptable to the popular magazines. Many of them were published, however, by Bill.

Hemingway was much interested in bullfighting and in 1926, with several friends, took the trip to Pamplona which he has described in *The Sun Also Rises.* The characters in that story are real enough—in fact so real most of them found it hard to forgive him. "Brett," who was furious at first, later relented. At one time all Montparnasse was talking of the "six characters in search of an author—with a gun!" I will tell more about "Mike" and "Brett" in a later chapter.

It was just after this trip that Hemingway started work on the novel. He was in Madrid, and the date was the twenty-first of July, his birthday. Hemingway was feeling his years, thought he was getting old or something, and was wondering why he had never written a novel. Well, why not write a novel, he thought, and there and then started to work. Within six weeks *The Sun Also Rises* was finished and on its way to a publisher.

Hemingway came to my bar frequently (he was no white-winer!) and we would have long conversations about boxing or he would tell me about bullfighting, in which I was much interested though I knew nothing about it. He has told me that he himself actually fought bulls at one time. On my night off we often went to boxing matches together, or if he had gone alone he would come to the bar afterward to tell me what he had seen. He would get so excited, sometimes, he would start sparring in the bar and almost knock someone over. At one time we were going to train together at a gymnasium in the rue Vandamme, but something happened and we never did. I think he went away about that time.

Hemingway learned boxing at the age of fifteen. One Christmas his father presented him with a course of fifteen lessons at the local gym. The managers, who operated the business as a racket, insisted on payment in advance for all the lessons. When a candidate presented himself for the first workout, the instructors so beat, mauled, and manhandled him he rarely returned a second time. But Hemingway, as soon as he could stand up again comfortably, returned for more. The instructors, seeing he was really serious about boxing, gave him a thorough course.

Hemingway is still a good fighter and demonstrated it the last time he was in Paris by landing a KO on another writer's chin in a bar argument.

Still another of this group was Ford Madox Ford, the English novelist, who came to my bars frequently. Ford was a great organizer of good times, first in his *bal musette* near the Place de la Contrescarpe and later in his own studio. The *bal musette* was a little workman's dance hall which Ford rented on Tuesdays and to which the Montparnasse crowd was invited. Music was furnished by a small Auvergnat orchestra and drinks could be bought at that bar. At first it was novel and amusing and everyone was gay, and there was a decidedly literary quality to it.

Ford once offered a prize for the best poem to be submitted to a jury before the next reunion at the dance hall. The prize was a freshly baked homemade cake. There were many contestants, as the cake was large. I was there on Ford's invitation the night the prize was to be awarded, watching the jury paw the manuscripts in one corner and the crowd eye the cake, which certainly looked good. Then the jury became more noisy! Finally they were shouting at each other! No decision could be reached and the wrangle went on and on. In fact it went on for days, until the cake had become so stale it ceased to be a prize and became a liability! It was awarded in the end to Bandy, the author of a fine work on Baudelaire, and everyone with strong teeth had a piece. In his best walrus manner Ford made a speech of presentation that was completely unintelligible, sounding something like "woof-woof and . . . aaaah . . . woof-woofus . . . who . . . whhhhhh . . . aaaaaah . . . whoof-whhhhhhhhhh!" Everyone said it was a good speech.

But Ford found it difficult to control his crowd, and in the end an undesirable element crept in that caused him to abandon the *bal musette* in favor of giant parties at his studio in the rue

Nôtre-Dame des Champs. Ford was making considerable money at that time and he spent much of it entertaining his Montparnasse friends with large quantities of the finest wines and liqueurs. He is a very generous man, who loves to entertain. Once, after a trip to America, he brought back many bottles of bootleg gin and whisky to show Montparnasse the meaning of strong "likker." He arranged a long table with the bootleg at one end and French cognac, wine, and liqueurs at the other. At first each guest tried the American bathtub gin and whisky in order to turn up his nose at it. "What terrible stuff!" they said. But by two in the morning the bootleg gin and whisky were all gone, while the French brandies and liqueurs had only been nibbled at.

When Ford occupied a villa at St. Tropez he had a feud with John Cox that caused much merriment in that gossipy old town. It seems that Ford raised a few chickens, but one by one they were killed by a mysterious hand. Ford was much disturbed, especially as he could not catch the killer. He knew the motive must be ill will, for the chickens were never stolen. He finally accused Cox, who indignantly denied it while the rest of St. Tropez laughed!

Bandy, the prizewinner mentioned previously, is a Virginian with strong convictions about Edgar Allan Poe. I remember a very heated discussion he had with Hiler at my bar one night that lasted until closing time, and even then I had to put them out. Bandy claimed that Poe must have lived in France to have written *The Murders in the Rue Morgue,* but Hiler insisted that so observing a man as Poe would never have written "then he raised a window," as he did in that story, if he had ever been in a French hotel! They became quite violent about it!

Montparnasse has had, at one time or another, most of the celebrated writers of the time, though some, like James Stevens, who wrote *The Crock of Gold,* have only stayed a short time. Stevens lived on the rue Campagne-Première and I used to see him in the Closerie des Lilas nearby. Once he left the manuscript of a new book on a table and walked out without remembering it. He did not miss it until a day or so later and then began a frantic search of Paris for what represented a year's work! He didn't remember having left it at the Closerie; he didn't remember having left it anywhere!

At the end of three or four days Stevens was frantic. The manuscript had simply vanished. To console himself he went to the Closerie for a drink. "Excuse me, sir," said the waiter, "did you leave a package of papers here the other day? I thought perhaps you had left them to be thrown away, but I was not sure, so I thought I'd ask you!" Stevens is reported to have kissed him on both cheeks, but I think that may be an exaggeration. Anyway, the waiter was surprised at the tip he received.

Sinclair Lewis, the American novelist, was another who stayed but a short time with us, but while there he caused much comment. His red head could usually be seen at the Dôme amid a group of the curious. He came into my bar once or twice but he was not friendly to barmen. In fact he was not friendly to Montparnasse, saying that most of us were a crowd of useless drunks. He took it out in an article on Harold Stearns, the author of *America and the Young Intellectual* and editor of *Civilization in the United States,* whom he called "the very father and seer of the Dôme" and "an authority on living without laboring." Stearns, in a well-worded reply justifying the Quarter, said, "The chief good point [of Montparnasse], of course, is that remotely, somehow, somewhere, even the dumbest American expatriates have been touched by the spiritual forces of French life." It is doubtful if Red Lewis, was, however.

Another article by Lewis in an American review described the suicide of Larry Murphy, which he presented as the ultimate fate of Montparnassians who were degenerating into utter futility. Larry would certainly have laughed to have read his obituary. It was such a misrepresentation of his character as I knew it! In another chapter I shall tell of the circumstances.

Hiler tells me of presenting Lewis to a young American negro who made pretense of being an intellectual. Hiler had been impressed with the struggle of this lad to educate himself and develop a full appreciation of modern artistic movements. When, however, the colored boy met Lewis, the best he could do was to wring his hand and say, "Yas, sah, I loves you' poetry!"

Bob McAlmon, in a recent letter, reminds me of "a Dôme night when Lewis . . . swore himself both a better stylist and psychologist than Flaubert and was silenced by a 'sit down, you're just a best-seller!'" No, the Quarter didn't like Mr. Lewis.

A white-winer of note was Gordon Craig, who liked us better. I saw him one time on the terrace of the Dôme, his big hat surrounded by a group of chattering, stagestruck women who wanted him to found a theater in Paris. Craig said nothing. He had no chance. Finally, during a brief lull, Hiler said, "I'd like to hear Mr. Craig talk for a change." Craig was pleased and they became friends forthwith.

Craig has a great liking for American jazz music. "The thing I want most at present," he said once, "is a complete collection of records by Ethel Waters."

He lived in Rapallo, as does Ezra Pound, though they did not seem to know each other at that time. Rapallo is a small place and they could hardly help seeing each other. "Yes, I live in Rapallo," said Craig. "I see Pound, but he's standoffish." Later Pound was reported to have said, "Craig is one of those damned snobbish Englishmen!"

Pound denies this, however, and wrote to *Esquire* that he "never said Craig was a snob. He can't help being an Englishman. Have known him since about 1912. Jimmie is correct in saying that Mr. Craig and I have not met in Rapallo, though."

Still another white-winer was Norman Douglas, who lived in the Quarter for a short time with his young Italian protégés, those beautiful lads he was so good to. Douglas was once a geologist, which accounts for the accurate geological descriptions in his books, and he still likes to talk about rocks and terrestrial formations with anyone who is informed.

Douglas, like Lytton Strachey, used to go to Paris once or twice a year to see a good American dentist. Which reminds me of something Gerald Heard once said: "Americans have abominably good teeth! Really it is very bad taste! No Englishman would have such white teeth! Americans go in for all that stupid dentrifice advertising stuff!"

Sisley Huddleston must not be forgotten in the Sylvia Beach group, for he is their historian and is said to have made a small fortune writing about the Montparnasse celebrities he has known. I hope I succeed as well, though of course I'll never have his style! Huddleston has in his day been a fighter, he told me at a party one time. Once, in a barroom fight in England, he knocked out the amateur champion of the British army! That must have been a long time ago.

Another chronicler of the great is Gertrude Stein, who, with her brother Leo, had been in the Quarter for many years before I arrived. Recently I have been reading her book *The Autobiography of Alice B. Toklas,* which is about herself and all the intellectuals. In one place she says she ("Alice" of course) has met but three geniuses in her life: Gertrude Stein, Pablo Picasso, and Alfred Whitehead. This reminds me of my father, whose name was also Jimmy Charters. Father always claimed there had been but three outstanding geniuses in the world, and in each case their initials were the same, namely J.C. The three geniuses were Julius Caesar, Jesus Christ, and Jimmy Charters!

There is no doubt Miss Stein has built an impressive reputation around herself, but there in Montparnasse they took her less seriously, though several of the young writers were sufficiently interested to help her try to find a publisher for some of her work. Rather more attention was given to Leo Stein, her brother, who, though deaf, had a great many admirers for the keenness of his criticisms and comments.

George Slocombe, with the flaming red beard that is known in all the capitals of Europe, was another writer about the Quarter, though he lived in Montmartre. To his friends he is far better known for his sea chanties, which he sings in a lusty voice.

One who did not even indulge in mild white whine was Cheever Dunning, the poet, who died several years ago. Cheever's order was always the same: an apple and a glass of coffee or milk—the typical opium smoker's diet. He was the champion thin man of Montparnasse, a great poker and bridge player, and a very likable person even though usually silent. He was a steady client of mine for years but I never heard him order a drink containing alcohol, which proves, I suppose, that the friendliness of the bars was a very real thing even without liquor.

A "character" who was a white-winer and well-known to the Quarter was old Daniel, black sheep of a wealthy Bordeaux family, former reporter for the *Intransigeant,* and gentleman jockey. He is famous for his amazing gestures and intricate stories, a habit of holding his cigarette between his thumb and forefinger, and the constant snapping of his fingers. *"Enfin, à la gaiété!"* (Well, anyway, here's to gaiety!) is a frequent remark of his. He always calls me his *soigneur,* his caretaker, or *l'homme en face,* the man opposite. He usually speaks French, but if he thinks someone at the bar is talking about him, he will come out with a typical American wisecrack that makes everyone laugh. He has, as a matter of fact, a very good knowledge of English and spends hours in the bars frequented by Anglo-Saxons. A grand old man is Daniel, and an essential part of the background of the Quarter. He takes rank with Pa Parslow, the oldest white-winer among us. Pa, though, finally returned to England after forty-eight years in Paris as a newspaperman. I have seen him many a time stand on a bridge over the Seine, look up and down the river, sigh, and say, "Ah, Jimmie, this is good enough for me. I will never go back."

Another I remember well was Tod Robbins, who loved to make very ferocious grimaces at me, making himself very tough and brutal, and then suddenly changing his face into his very winning smile. Tod is the author of *The Unholy Three* and a one-time prizefighter. He certainly was good with his fists and had one of the most beautiful physiques I have ever seen. "I keep fit," he told me, "because I go south once a year or to the seaside where I do nothing but box, train, and play tennis."

Tod was, nevertheless, a little man and several times I was asked, "Who is that poor little lonely fellow who looks so sad?"

Tod told me of winning a short-story prize a few years earlier, offered by an American physical-culture magazine.

"It's too bad," said the editor when he met Tod, "that you are not a good physical specimen so we might run an article about you with photos."

"What!" said Tod, pulling off his coat and shirt, "What did you say?" The photos were published!

Tod, incidentally, is the grandson of the famous steeplechase rider, Clary Robbins.

There was a whole group of white-winers who spent their summers in Brittany. All of them were favorite clients of mine, such as Jimmy Lane, a former British army officer, a distinguished person who spoke perfect German and French; Dobson, the English sculptor of note; Cecil Maitland with his monocle and air of superiority; and Peggy Scott, who was then Peggy Cummings, wife of the poet.

But Tommy Earp, writer and heir to the Earp brewery fortune, stands out particularly in my mind. I can see his close-cropped head with six hairs in front that stood straight up, a book always under his arm. He would read for a couple of hours at a time while sitting at the bar. Tommy always had a certain respect for me of which I was very proud. He used to say, "James, you are most efficient!" It was in reference to what he considered my prowess in dealing with women.

But the leaders of the Brittany crowd were Ferdinand Tuohy and Kinko. Theirs was a romance that stirred Montparnasse deeply. *"Je vous suivrai partout!"*—I will follow you everywhere—Kinko said to Tuohy, and she proved it in the end. She told me that if anything happened to Tuohy she would commit suicide at once.

Tuohy and Kinko had walked or bicycled over many parts of France, seeking the spots off the beaten track, particularly in Brittany. Kinko, who was a white-winer of note, was quite happy to enjoy the simpler pleasures. When she was tired she would say, "Now let's have a piece of white wine."

Tuohy is the son of a well-known journalist and himself a very capable man in that profession. He and I were great friends. "James," he used to say most seriously, "do you know that the automobile is the cause of civilization's downfall? Do you? And do you know that if France did away with Pernod and all drinks of that kind, they would have no need for Devil's Island? Do you?" Well, I didn't, not in my profession; but that is no matter.

One day in Brittany Tuohy fell off a bridge and Kinko jumped to save him. There was no hesitation in following him; she had no fear. Hitting a rock, I believe, she broke her spine and died shortly after. Over her grave should have been cut the words *Je vous suivrai partout!*

Curtis Moffat, the world's most English American, and his wife, Iris Tree, who is the daughter of Sir Beerbohm Tree, were familiar figures in those days. Iris Tree was the first to wear her fine golden hair in that straight Jeanne d'Arc style that later became so popular.

Moffat must have been educated at Oxford to have acquired such an accent. In fact, it was more exaggerated than any Oxford accent I have heard before or since, and he was very serious about it. He wore a Gordon Craig hat to set it off.

Once Curtis was asked how he liked Sir Beerbohm Tree as Shylock. "Oh, ah—funny without being vulgah!" On another occasion a group was seated at one end of the room and Florence Gilliam, a former light of Greenwich Village, suggested they join some friends farther down. "Let's join the gang," she said. "Ah, gang, gang? What is a gang?" said Moffat.

Cedric Morris, who wore the corduroy clothes of a French workman, and his friend Arthur Lett-Haines were frequently with this crowd. They were likable young men and I am glad that Cedric has made a success of his painting. They had a poodle called Miss Boggs of which they were very fond. They kept her on a leash at all times and they insisted that the Miss in her name was no mere politeness. One day Miss Boggs ran away and when she came back she was Mrs. Boggs with a large litter of puppies.

One night Gene MacCown, the painter, gave a party in his studio for the whole crowd which lasted most of the night. Nancy Cunard was the one who told me about it. She said Norman Douglas told interesting stories of his travels in Africa, while the Princess Violet Murat went from guest to guest, slapping each on the back with her Russian martinet. Douglas did not appreciate this. Guevara, the Chilean painter and amateur boxer, who married one of the Misses Guinness, was also a guest. Even Curtis Moffat was impressed by the talent present.

ABOUT DRINKS

The first thing I know about drinking is that I myself cannot do it. One or two strong drinks and I am on a rampage for the rest of the day—if not a couple of days, if not a couple of weeks! And so I almost never drink. I regret that this should be the case with me, because I like to drink and because I find it good policy to drink with my customers. I notice that my receipts at the end of the day are always higher if I drink a little with my friends.

Fortunately for the bar business, most people are not like me. No man ever has the capacity he thinks he has, but, drinking slowly, most of the Quarterites could consume quite a number of strong drinks without particularly showing it.

I always give everyone the same strength drink, unless I think he has reached the stage of abandon or unless I know he has a weak capacity like mine. Some barmen give their friends stronger drinks than those who drop in by chance, but I think this is a mistake.

The safest way to drink is the French way, and if you stick to this formula you can never go wrong: before dinner not more than two cocktails or aperitifs; with the meal a good wine properly served; after the meal, coffee and one or two liqueurs; then stop. Such a system will make you gay, light, and clearheaded the next day, and you will enjoy yourself without danger of excess. If you are obliged to continue drinking during the afternoon or evening, switch to light beer. Fortunately for bars, Anglo-Saxons always agree with me when I tell them this, but they never follow the advice.

One of the great helps to the bar business in France was

prohibition in America. The French winegrowers may complain that their exports were cut in two, but the bar and café owners reaped a big harvest. To a certain class of Americans, drinking to excess became an obligation; no party was a success without complete intoxication of the guests, and it takes a lot of liquor at six francs a drink to intoxicate some Americans!

New arrivals from England or America almost always started on Pernod. I think it was the color. Pernod is one of a dozen trade names for a synthetic substitute for absinthe. The latter has, of course, been banned in France since war days, but so powerful is the substitute that the Chamber of Deputies has actually considered bringing back the real absinthe and banning the substitutes! The French workmen called it *lait de tigre*—tiger's milk! It is really the same sort of thing as the imitation absinthe which is made in New Orleans. It is a clear, pale green liquid as you pour it in the glass, but when you add water to it, it turns a milky, greenish color. The taste is that of licorice.

One of the first sights to attract the newly arrived tourist is a number of dignified old gents sitting on the café terrace drinking this milky liquid with the entrancing color. I will try one, he thinks, and try one he does. It tastes sweet, and it tastes mild. Fine, he thinks. In Paris do as the Parisians. He doesn't realize that a Frenchman only takes *one,* and then only just before a meal. This he sits with for an hour, taking a sip now and then while he talks or reads his paper. But the Englishman drinks one after another, quietly but steadily, while the American gulps his down. Well, they both learn! At the end of a month most of them switch to something milder, usually cocktails, fizzes, or other fancy drinks. In the end they come to plain distillations, like whisky and brandy. The Anglo-Saxons never take to liqueurs, as the French do.

It has been my experience that painters and photographers are the biggest drinkers and that they go in for Pernod, Picon, and Mandarin in a large way. They are always the loudest and most conspicuous in any gathering, too. The hangers-on, those who do nothing but enjoy themselves as best they can around bars, come second in consumption. The next-heaviest drinkers are the journalists, some of whom have fine capacities for beer, whisky and soda, or straight brandy.

Save me from a bar full of sculptors, for they are almost always very depressed when drinking. The writers, too, are very quiet, but rather because they are reserved than depressed, I think. Perhaps it is silly to make such classifications, for there are always exceptions, but I have remarked to myself on these things for several years.

I think the safest drink is good Scotch whisky, straight or with plain water. Soda water in any drink makes it go to your head faster and often gives you a headache the next day. Brandy, which is more of a stimulant, is bad for the nerves. All the heavy brandy drinkers I can think of in the old days are now two feet under the ground, while the heavy whisky drinkers are still going strong.

Gin is a good drink, too, I think, especially for an aperitif, as in a martini cocktail. Straight gin is a bit raw for the stomach. But stay away from the strong French aperitifs which are synthetically made, or from the heavy French wines that contain coffee and chicory, for they will ruin your stomach in the end if you drink them regularly.

One of the best before-dinner drinks that I know of is a glass of good cold beer, which makes you hungry and prepares the stomach for the meal. Beer is excellent for the morning after the night before, too.

Champagne is also a good pick-me-up, or tomato juice, or an oyster cocktail. For some people a prairie oyster does the trick, though others cannot stand the thought of it. For the stomach, take a bromo-seltzer, bicarbonate of soda, or a Fernet Branca. *Menthe* or a cup of hot soup are good, too.

Of course, the best way is to avoid a hangover, which is simple enough if you follow certain principles. Mixtures of any kind will intoxicate faster than twice the amount of the same drink, and especially when they involve distillations of both grapes and grain.

And now comes a question that I have been asked many times, often for a purpose: What drinks are aphrodisiac? I do not hesitate on this score. They are Pernod and the other French synthetic aperitif drinks (Amer-Picon and Mandarin), for both men and women. Women are also susceptible to *menthe* and green Chartreuse.

I must tell you of a cocktail I invented while I was at the Dingo that had a powerful effect on some of the Quarterites. It was made with ⅓ cognac, ⅙ Pernod, ⅙ Amer-Picon, ⅙ Mandarin, and ⅙ sweet cherry brandy. This mixture was shaken thoroughly in a cocktail shaker and then either drunk straight or diluted with a little soda. Either way the taste is pleasant and not strong, but two stiff drinks of it will have some surprising effects!

One group of men who had had several of these rushed out of the Dingo and were later found asleep in the trees that formerly shaded the Dôme. Another was clinging to the crossbar of the lamppost, also sound asleep. The police dislodged the sleepers only after great effort, and then with the aid of a hook-and-ladder company. They were aloft more than four hours! Another time, a man who had imbibed several returned to his studio and wrecked everything in it without afterward remembering how he had done it.

On women this drink had the effect of causing them to undress in public, and it often kept me busy wrapping overcoats around nude ladies! But even knowing this did not prevent some of the feminine contingent from asking for the Jimmie Special. I wish I had a hundred francs for every nude or seminude lady I've wrapped up during the best Montparnasse days!

In the end Mrs. Wilson, the wife of the owner of the Dingo, forbade me to make any more Jimmie Specials. Mrs. Wilson liked to keep the moral tone as high as possible.

Let me tell you an amusing drinking story that was told me by one of the participants. Two writers, both of them known, staged a pretty big night of drinking in celebration of something not recorded. They went from bar to bar all night until six o'clock in the morning found them at the Halle aux Vins (central wine market of Paris) somewhat the worse for wear, but still keeping their heads up. On leaving a café near the market, they were amazed to see twenty or thirty flame-colored birds walking leisurely up the street.

"My God!" said one of them to his friend. "Do you see what I see? Do you see them?"

"Yes," gasped his friend. "Yes! Red! Do you see them? We've—we've got the d.t.'s!" And then following the flamingos were a flock of pelicans, ludicrously ambling along.

"You're right! I never had d.t.'s before! My God I feel strange!" Suddenly behind them came the vibrant strains of a bagpipe, and turning they beheld three Scots in kilts. The writers almost took to their heels! They covered their eyes for a moment, but the birds and the Scots were still there when they removed their hands. "I really felt like jumping into the Seine," one of them told me later, "but I was paralyzed with fear."

It was fully ten minutes before they realized that they were just outside the zoological gardens and that the flamingos and pelicans were simply being transferred from one garden to another. The Scots were part of a group that had been sent to France for some parade. When all was explained, my friends joined with the Scots, who had also been spending the night in bars, and the party was continued. Later they wound up at the studio of another Montparnassian. There they decided to plant a tree, to commemorate the occasion, in the garden of the *concierge*. She, however, did not appreciate the joke and finally called her husband, who threw them out, bagpipes and all!

Of the many drinking stories one hears in a bar my favorite is the one about the Cockney women told by Courteney Haynes, New York social-registerite.

"'Ere," she said, on coming into a pub, "Give us two w'iskies for two ly-dies."

"*Two* ly-dies?" said the bartender, looking over the rail. "But I don't see but one o' you!"

"That's right! That's right! The other ly-dy is restin' in the guttah!"

Then there is the one about the man who comes into the bar and asks for a whisky and soda.

"And make it strong, Jimmie! I need a strong one before the big fight."

I serve him and he takes it like a man.

"Another, Jimmie. Give me another before the big fight."

After I have served him six or seven drinks in rapid succession, I lean over to him.

"Excuse me, sir, but where is this big fight going to take place? I'd like to see it if possible."

"Oh, you'll see it all right, because it's going to take place right now between you and me when you find out I have no money to pay!"

Drunks are funny! I remember particularly one evening in the Dingo when the bar was not as crowded as usual. I wish I could have taken a photograph of it. At one end of the bar sat a man known to the Quarter as "Gin Fizz," who had fallen asleep in a large plate of tomato soup, his head right in the bowl! Next to him sat a very wealthy Englishwoman, her feet on another stool, her furs dangling, her hat over one eye—also sound asleep. Beside her on the floor another woman rested in slumber on the bar rail. And so on around the bar. I would wake them up, one by one, and try to give them soda to get sober, but it was no use. Once awake, each would cry, "Another drink, Jimmie! God! Give me another drink!" I gave them drinks that were mostly water and eventually they all came to. I took Gin Fizz downstairs and washed the tomato soup out of his hair with some difficulty.

Fortunately we had some clients who never or rarely drank to excess, and these tended to have a good influence on the others.

Montparnasse was mostly talk, as I have implied before. We had some excellent talkers, sincere, amusing, fantastic, or simply incredible. Like talkers the world over, their main subject was themselves. Captain Walker, with his air of distinction, arm in arm with a British major wearing a bright blue monocle, stands out in my memory particularly. I can see them walking down the Boulevard du Montparnasse as though they owned the place and it had been in the family for generations.

Walker was a pseudo-English officer with a game leg, a typical adventurer of the remittance-man variety. His stories of his own exploits were so exaggerated as to arouse wonder at his courage in telling them.

"You know," he used to say, "I took my destroyer in 1914, when the war broke out, straight up to Scapa Flow and beat the Germans practically single-handed. My crew and I simply forced them into hiding there. Later the rest of the British navy came and kept them bottled up for the remainder of the war. This is a matter of record which you will find in the Admiralty archives.

"Later, you know, in 1917, I took my destroyer—yes, the same destroyer—and made the fastest crossing on water that has ever been made from England to America. It was three days, five hours, and forty-five minutes. I went right to Washington and told President Wilson that he must declare war. He was forced to agree, and declared war that same day. Yes, you know, you will find all that in the Admiralty archives."

He told many stories of his years in India before the war, when, according to his account, he was the real power behind the viceroy.

"Once," he said, "I was visiting the maharaja of Indore. We had finished our dinner and were sitting on the terrace of his palace from which stretched an expanse of forest. The maharaja was telling me of the secret political movements of the country. 'I hope,' he said, 'that we will not be interrupted during the liqueurs, for I have an exciting tale to tell you.'

"He had started his tale when suddenly I heard a slight noise behind me. Turning, I found myself face-to-face with a huge Bengal tiger—the man-eating kind, you know. I knew the maharaja must not be interrupted, so without calling his attention to the intruder, I fixed the beast with my eye, looking him through and through. Then very gently I said 'whoof!' and he raced off into the jungle again! Thus the maharaja's story was never interrupted for even a moment."

Captain Walker's air of superiority was magnificent. He was superior to everything, yet always agreeable to those around him, especially if they bought him drinks. I remember one time when the news had just arrived of a giant earthquake in Japan, a colossal disaster. Walker, on being informed of it, said, "Oh well, boys will be boys, you know!"

Walker was usually on the point of making large sums of money, and occasionally he did make quite a bit, always by some deal in antiques, real estate, or documents. His adventures, considerably sentimentalized, have been told in Maryse Rutledge's book, *The Sad Adventurers*.

Captain Walker drank so much Pernod in the end that he dried up his alimentary canal and died a very painful death.

One of the mystery men of those days was an American named Leaming, who claimed to have been a monk in Russia and was in Paris simply for a rest from "monking." He loved to tell weird stories which he always insisted were true. I remember one that everyone talked of at the time.

"In 1919," Leaming said, "a Russian princess of great beauty died in Paris in her twenty-third year. She had escaped from the revolution in Russia with her life and her jewels, but all her relatives had been murdered by the communists. So saddened was she by this loss and her ghastly adventures that she literally pined away.

"At her death her will was opened and it contained a most curious bequest. I have seen the will and I assure you of the truth of my statements. It provided that a large vault should be built in Père Lachaise cemetery. She herself was to be placed, totally nude, in a coffin made entirely of glass. The coffin was to be sealed hermetically in such a way that her body would be preserved in perfect condition for many years.

"All this has been done. The vault is built, and, as she requested, the coffin has been placed in it on end so that the body seems that of a lovely woman standing in a natural position.

"The remainder of the vault has been furnished with a fine bed, table, bookshelves and books, and even a bath with running hot and cold water. Is it not remarkable? But I can vouch for the truth of all I tell you.

"And now comes the most curious part of all. Her fortune of well over a million francs is left to a man who shall pass one entire year within the vault, along with the lovely ivory-skinned lady. He will not be alone, for her eyes are open and they seem to follow one to every part of the room, I am told.

"During that year the lucky man is to have whatever he chooses in the way of books and phonograph records; he may work on sculpture, painting or writing, or anything he chooses. He may have what materials he likes. There is no window in the vault, but ample air and light is provided by a skylight. In the door is a small sliding passage by which his food will be brought to him three times a day. He may order to his heart's desire of meat or drink.

"Is it not wonderful? What a chance to do serious creative work, what a chance to concentrate on new ideas!

"The lucky man will even be allowed to take half an hour's exercise in a garden nearby which is closed to everyone except himself and his guard. He may not speak to the guard, for the latter is deaf and dumb. All communication must be done by writing.

"And, near the door of the vault, is an electric button. It is the button of freedom. The man who lives there has but to push the button and at once the guard will come, open the door, and give him his liberty. But of course, if he leaves before the end of one year, he forfeits his claim to the inheritance.

"Only two have tried it, a Dutchman who stayed two months and later went insane, and a Russian who stayed but one night. Both said that the terrible part was the night, in the dark, when the body of the nude girl seemed to take on a luminous quality.

"I myself am thinking of entering the vault. I have talked to the executor, a lawyer with Offices in the Champs Élysées. I should return to Russia, but perhaps I shall enter the vault instead. It offers an unparalleled opportunity for meditation."

He told this story far better than I have, I fear. The listeners were at least half convinced, if not wholly so. Some even thought of asking for the address of the lawyer, that they might try for the million francs.

Another artist with speech was the poet Maxwell Bodenheim, notorious for his colored berets and his easy but eloquent declarations of love. Of the berets he had a blue one, a pink one, a green one, and several other shades. He would change them several times a day. In New York he had entered a suicide pact and the girl in question had died while he had survived. He came to Montparnasse to "forget" and was always talking about the "poor girl who died for me—she was so beautiful!"

Captain Vail was an adventurer who, after the war, purchased secondhand airplanes, fixed them up so they would fly (once, anyway), and sold them. He would deliver them himself, in proof of the fact that they were airworthy. Vail was one of the heaviest brandy drinkers I have ever known. "You haven't been anywhere until you've had the d.t.'s," he used to say. "Those are real travels!"

Bob Brown was another who had led a life of adventure, though in a different way. He had been a book collector and dealer, a dispenser of ideas which were sold by mail order from two dollars to ten dollars each, a newspaperman, a short-story writer of the one-every-day kind, a Wall Street financier, again a book dealer, a magazine publisher in Rio de Janeiro. In Montparnasse he was the inventor of a reading machine. The latter was an ingenious substitute for the bulky books with which our libraries are encumbered.

Bob used to tell stories of Frank A. Munsey, the newspaper owner. "Munsey was an Anglophile. I met him once at the Hotel Carlton in London. Later I dropped my middle name, Carlton. Somebody else told me he had an idée fixe that England, America, and Germany must all adopt the French franc as their currency unit because tipping a franc instead of a shilling, quarter, or mark would have reduced the cost of living nearly twenty percent at that time!"

MASTER RACONTEUR

One of the most loved and greatly appreciated storytellers of Montparnasse was Les Copeland, an old-time Westerner with a gift for repartee and old songs.

I first met Les when I worked in the Hole-in-the-Wall, on the Right Bank, and he was playing at Harry's New York Bar. He always stood at one end of my bar, a big black hat on his head, Western fashion, a cigar in his mouth, and his sharp eyes taking in everything. He had a slight cast in one eye which gave his face a peculiar expression. Every once in a while he would shout, "I'm a sheriff from Arizona!" and then laugh in great, loud guffaws. Pedro, the barman, didn't know what to make of him, but I thought he was a fine man. Later, in Montparnasse, I knew him much better and we often went on drinking parties together. Les was always in demand for parties because he told such good stories.

Les started his career as a pianist in the high and wide mining camps of Goldfields and Bonanza, in the saloons "where men are pure gold and women melt them down." Les always had about him that aura of "see what the boys in the back room will have," the true Western type.

Les's weapon throughout life, and he was about fifty-five when he left Montparnasse, though he looked but forty, was his wit. A ready response to anything that was said was a perfect protection in this world, he claimed.

Playing the piano and working as a billiard marker, he had hoboed his way through every state in the Union, as well as most of England and France. He was an expert on accents, and claimed this helped him greatly in the States.

"I used to take a train," he told me once, "a freight train, you know, riding the rods, and get off when I came to a likely town. The first day I would wander around a new town and find out the nationality of the owner of the best joint there. If he was an Irishman I'd bring out my best Irish accent, and soon we'd be talking over conditions in Dublin and cursing the English as though we'd just left Cork that day. Or if he was a German I would go in for a long appreciation of sausage in all its forms. I almost always got a job, even if someone else had to be fired."

As a pianist and singer at the Jockey in Montparnasse, Les was a great success from the moment of his arrival, for he knew all the words to such songs as "Frankie and Johnnie," "Stackerlee," "There Was a Young Cowboy," and literally dozens of others of the West. When he played "The Chicago Stockyards in 1909" with its old-fashioned ragtime, trotter bass, it would make the old-timers fairly weep in their drinks.

Hilaire Hiler, who had made a collection of Western songs, was very much interested in Les's comments on them. For instance, Les insisted that the original name of "Frankie and Johnnie" was "Frankie and Albert."

"Kansas City," he said, "had a district known as the Bottoms, full of railroad yards, packing houses, tanneries, factories, with a big colored population and a famous tenderloin or red-light district. Frankie was a real girl who lived there. Albert was her sweetheart, well-known in the underworld, a celebrity as it were, and a sensationalist to the extent of driving spotted polo ponies, tandem style, to a hightrap, with two thoroughbred bulldogs beside him. Always conspicuous, he had quite a following amongst the fair sex, and being constantly overcome by temptation, was unfaithful to the girlfriend. The result was that he stopped a couple of slugs. The tragedy is explained in the song.

"In singing the song today so many people speak of Frankie's 'forty-four gun.' It should be 'forty-one gun,' because in those days

Colt manufactured something between a thirty-eight and a forty-four. A forty-one is just about the kind of a gun a gal *would* carry."

In reference to the "Engineer's Song," Les said, "This was originally sung by the colored brakeman and fireman on the old K.C. Railroad, now part of the Frisco system, running between Birmingham, Alabama, and Memphis, Tennessee. The song later became known as 'Casey Jones.'"

Regarding the song "Stackerlee," the late Palmer Jones once told Hiler that this song originated in Memphis shortly after the murder of the notorious gambler, Billy Lyons, by his best friend and comrade, William "Stacker" Lee. The word "stacker" doubtless refers to his habits when playing cards. Les, in commenting on the same song, said, "Stackerlee was no doubt a real bad man. This is a song about a levee gambler in St. Louis who had a heart as hard as granite and was so tough you couldn't manicure him with an emery wheel. He carried razors for social purposes and his glance was like an automatic drill."

Les also said that "Willie the Weeper" came from the "Hop Song," the first character song of the underworld that he ever heard. It was composed by an entertainer in Cripple Creek, Colorado, by the name of Guy Hallie.

Les was very independent, especially when he had been drinking. It was not a mean streak; it was simply that he followed his desires without thinking. Sometimes he would walk out of the Jockey in the middle of a song, a bottle of whisky or brandy tucked under his arm. Once he and the Countess Eileen de Vismes, an English girl who was one of my best friends, had been doing some fancy drinking at a small café until there was a big pile of saucers to be paid for. In France, you know, the saucer under your glass is marked with the price of the drink. Every time you order an additional drink, you are given an additional saucer! Neither had any money, so Les left Eileen in hock while he set about raising some. Well, Les soon forgot about Eileen. She simply passed out of his mind and might be sitting there yet if she hadn't persuaded a waiter to get Les and bring him back.

Les, incidentally, was very generous, always spending what money he had on other people. When he wished to borrow money, he had ways of asking I had never heard before. I would be at the bar and Les would come around, stand at one end, order a drink and wait. Then I would hear a soft voice say, "Jimmie, when nobody's looking, slip me a century!" A century was a hundred francs. Or sometimes he would ask for a "sawbuck," five hundred francs. Then he would wait a moment, look around carefully.

"All right, Jimmie, there never was a better moment!" When I gave him the money, he would say, "Jimmie, you're a little beauty, you're a pippin!" Once he got three hundred-franc notes out of me in ten minutes with this line. It was irresistible.

Although Les did a great deal of drinking, his health was excellent. Once in a while he would decide to go on the wagon, but he found it difficult.

"You know, Jimmie," he said, "they give you too much to drink with meals over here. They give you about ten or fifteen beers for lunch!"

His great recreation was walking, and he tramped for miles every fine day. Then, after a long walk, he would buy a bag of fruit, jump in a taxi, and tell the driver to go wherever he pleased. Les ate great quantities of fruit, and also was fond of grass and flowers. Once at the Falstaff, Eileen gave him a big bouquet of flowers which he ate, one by one, in about ten minutes.

Les could have made plenty of money as an entertainer, but he would not exploit himself. He wanted just enough to keep him in fruit and drinks and he was happy. During his years in Paris he was three times called to London to entertain the Prince of Wales, but he preferred the company of artists and travelers, people who had knocked around a bit.

"There's a lot of good fellows follow the würzburger," he said, "and they're just my kind of people. They can write their own tickets. You know what the mule said, boy, 'back to the cactus.'"

The last phrase refers to one of his stories about a mule who lived with many other wild mules on the arid deserts of Arizona, keeping body and soul together with the food gleaned from the sparse and prickly cactus. One day a stallion came along, a fine big horse with glossy coat and sprightly step.

"Hello, mule," he said, "what do you live on?" and the stallion looked at the mule's shaggy coat full of dust.

"Why, I live on the cactus, like other mules around here," said the mule.

"You poor thing! You come with me, mule. I'll show you how to live."

"OK," said the mule. So off they went. They traveled for three days, and the stallion was surprised that the mule could run so fast, but he didn't say anything. Finally, at the end of the third day, when they were well into Colorado, they came to a big field of clover through which ran a small brook of clear, cool, fresh water. On one side was a barn, with straw, oats, electric fans for hot weather, stoves for cold weather, in fact everything a horse or mule could desire.

"Here we are," said the stallion, "now enjoy yourself."

So for three days the mule ate clover, slept on straw, drank the fresh water.

"How do you like it?" said the stallion, finally.

"OK," said the mule.

Another two or three days went by.

"How do you like it now?" said the stallion.

"Well . . . OK," said the mule. "There's only one thing bothers me. Have you got any mares?"

"You know," said the stallion, "yesterday I found a pasture over there full of bluegrass, the sweet kind they have in Kentucky. We'll go over there and try it."

"I didn't ask about no bluegrass," said the mule, "I asked if you had any mares."

"Well . . . well, no!"

"OK," said the mule, turning on his heel. "I guess it's back to the cactus for me. So long!"

Les's stories would fill a book! There was one about Arkansas that I liked particularly. Two farmers, in the back country of that lazy land, had been holding up a fence for some two or three hours, one on either side. Finally they decided to indulge in a little conversation.

"Say," said the one on the outside of the fence, pointing toward some hogs near the barn, "them there hawgs o' yourn is pretty thin."

"Yeah," said the other, "but I reckon they'll fatten up."

"Yeah?" said the first, "What do yo feed 'em on?"

"Falfi," said the second.

"Say, you won't fatten them hawgs in ten years on falfi!"

"Aw, what's time to a hawg!"

Unfortunately, in writing this story, Les's drawling imitation and pantomime are missing.

Another story is of two Pullman porters, an old-timer who had retired and a younger man who had been on the trains for only three or four years.

"Say," said the old-timer, "I bet I know'd every boardin' house you every stayed in when you was workin' on de trains. For instance, when you was on the B & M you stayed in Boston at ole Ma Chandler's Homelike, just near de North station, didn't you?"

"No, sir," said the other, "I didn't stop in no Ma Chandler's Homelike. I stopped in a cathouse."

"Oh, you did? Well . . . hum! Well, anyway I know'd where you stayed when you was in Philadelphia when you was working on the B & O. I know sure this time. You stayed at Philly Green's Open Kitchen on 17th and Lombard, now didn't you?"

"No sir, not me. I didn't stop in no Open Kitchen. I stopped in a cathouse."

"Well, say, that's funny. But how about de Chicago end? I bet you stopped at de Elite which old Saddle Jones runs, just behind de stockyards, didn't you?"

"No, I didn't stop in no Elite. I allus stopped in a cathouse, I tell you."

"Allus? How come you allus stopped in a cathouse?"

"Cheaper."

"Cheaper?"

"Sure, I stayed with relatives!"

Les had a reply to everything. Once, when asked by some new arrival what he did for a living, he said he was a jockey.

"But you're too heavy to be a jockey!"

"Well, you see I'm a jockey for elephants, and I'm just on my way to Delhi, India, for the New Jersey Sweepstakes!"

I wish I could remember more of Les's Western expressions, many of which were unknown to even the Americans in Montparnasse. For instance, he would never ask for a drink, but would say, "Jimmie, pour out my bread-and-butter, please," and this would mean a brandy and soda.

Les was last heard of as an entertainer in the very smart "Willows" in Reno, Nevada, in the early part of 1933. A letter to him there was returned with the notation, *No longer resident here. Left no forwarding address.* That was Les, all right! He always moved on in that sudden manner, without a plan, and without an address.

THE SUN ALSO SINKS

Of all the romances of Montparnasse, none ever gripped the imagination of the Quarterites as much as the one partially described in Ernest Hemingway's novel, *The Sun Also Rises*. For "Mike" and "Brett," the hero and heroine of the novel, were based on actual people. To give their real names would be pointless, and in any case I promised "Mike's" mother that I would not, for it would reflect on a very fine old Scotch family long prominent in British history.

Brett, too, came from a good family. Quite young she had Brett, too, came from a good family. Quite young she had married an English lord, but it was all a mistake from the first and they were soon separated. Shortly after that she met Mike in London.

Of all my friends in Montparnasse, Mike is the one I liked best. I liked Brett, too, but we never had quite the same understanding between us. Mike's father died while he was still a young man, leaving him a goodly sum of money upon his reaching his majority. Mike managed to spend that money in very short order, and thereafter received an allowance from his mother, just enough to live on modestly.

But Mike, lovable as he was, became quite irresponsible. There was no atom of meanness in him, but he ran up bills without a thought of where the money would come from. If he had money, he spent it generously on his friends. If he didn't have it, he spent it anyway. He knew and others knew that some day he would have a big fortune. That seemed excuse enough.

When Mike and Brett came to Paris they lived in a continual round of parties, entertainment, and good times. They were very much in love, and as a result everyone treated them with special consideration and attention. They were frequently in my bar and I came to know them both very well.

Mike was very proud of Brett, and often he would sit in the back of the room watching her while she talked with friends at the bar. "James, she is a marvelous girl," he would say. "James, if you produce the piano, I will produce the pianist." For Brett was an excellent musician. Mike would sit back there as long as Brett was enjoying herself, but woe to any man who laid a hand on her, for in a bound he would be at the bar.

Mike had many phrases which seemed affected to some, but he always said them with great dignity and yet with a twinkle in his eye. "James"—every sentence addressed to me started with my name pronounced in a grand manner—"James, let us have some wine of England," by which he meant pale ale. "Wine of Scotland" was whisky and soda, and "wine of France" was brandy at the bar or red wine at the table. If he moved from one place at the bar to another, he would say, "James, how is it my drink is not opposite me?" When he was ready to leave, he would say, "James, have your aide-de-camp conduct me to my carriage," which meant that I was to find his hat and coat.

Brett attracted more people to herself than did Mike, for she had a more pleasing personality. Mike was often annoyed by others, and he would say, "James, tell the ladies and gentlemen that I do not wish to be annoyed. Conduct them to their carriage, if any."

But Brett had a good word for everyone and she was always a lady, no matter what happened. She dressed neatly in somewhat masculine clothes, her bobbed head erect, her eyes bright, even when she might be feeling very groggy after a night of drinking. I knew when she was feeling bad only by a little wan smile that she never used at other times.

They made a fine couple. But then began the trouble that ruined Mike's life and certainly made Brett very unhappy. Brett had obtained a divorce that she might marry Mike, but at the last moment he changed his mind and shifted his affections to an American girl, much to everyone's surprise. We could not understand it, and I don't understand it now. However, outsiders never understand other people's personal relationships. Mike and Brett had known each other for five or six years; then suddenly things went wrong, that's all.

Mike did not stay long with his American girl, who had no great affection for him, as Brett had had. Soon Mike was around the bars, usually alone or with men friends, and nearly always without money. I gave him credit, partly because I liked him very much and partly because I felt sure he would pay me someday. At one time he owed me eight thousand francs, which is a great deal for one poor barman to carry. Sometimes I would try to stop his credit, and then he would say, "James, I feel frightfully rich!" At the same time he would rattle a wad of toilet paper in his pocket to make it sound like five-pound bank notes. I was often taken in by the sound of those notes!

In those days Mike and Brett were very strained in their relations, yet both frequented the Trois et As bar. Mike was indeed poor, and for a while had no place to sleep, so Madame Camille allowed him to stretch out in the bar on two chairs with a roll of bread for a pillow!

In the meantime Brett had met an American, and later married him. Today she lives in Greenwich Village, I am told.

After he broke with Brett, Mike was never the same. He was bothered with constant headaches, and complained that he could not sleep at night. Also he wanted feminine company now and then, but he would not make the effort to be agreeable to the girls he knew. He would say, "James, produce a lady!" I would reply that there were many on the Boulevard du Montparnasse and in the big cafés. "James, they are not ladies. No, James, get me a lady!"

But life became more and more difficult with so little money. Mike's debts began to overtake him, and finally, in a movement of desperation, he gave a bad check for five thousand francs to a hotel. The hotel complained and Mike was on the verge of arrest. He came to the Falstaff, somewhat bewildered and rather frightened, I think. It was a farewell drink, for Flossie Martin and Captain Porterfield put him on the train for England. The police were watching his hotel for him, but he saw them in time and dashed for the station in a taxi.

Mike's mother, who was very fond of him, was quite horrified by the escapade and determined to take radical action. So, under the influence of some liquid persuasion, Mike was started on his way to South Africa, "to the colonies," which English families always think a magic cure for black sheep.

Mike realized what was happening by the time he reached London, but he had no money to go elsewhere, so he went to Dublin and thence to Cape Town. Still Mike had very little money. Such a condition must be cured. So he invented a little story about a rich farm he had just procured, a good money-making proposition. When he had sold "shares" in it totaling two thousand pounds to some friends, they investigated and Mike made his escape back to England.

During his stay in South Africa he had received a bad cut on the lip in an automobile accident, which left a permanent scar.

In the meantime his mother had arranged things in Paris through the English ambassador, and Mike was allowed to return to France.

One evening Mike came to the bar with a serious look on his face. "James," he said, "my mother is going to pay all my bills, and I am giving her an idea of what I owe. I will start with you. How much do I owe you?" I laughed at him, for I thought it was another game to get additional credit. But Mike had a letter with him and I guess he was serious. We discussed it and he put the letter back in his pocket. Then he went out with a taxi driver friend of his.

This taxi man and Mike had had a strange sort of friendship for several years. The man, who lived in the Batignolles quarter, was very good to Mike, often driving him around in his taxi on credit, taking care of Mike when he was tight, even taking care of Mike's money. Mike once gave him ten thousand francs to keep for him when he was on his way to a party in Montmartre.

For the next several days Mike did not come near my bar, and I later learned that he had spent this time in the apartment of a woman who was known to use drugs. Whether Mike indulged in the drugs at her suggestion or not I do not know. Right after the war he had used drugs, but had given up the habit under Brett's influence. Now, perhaps, he slipped into it again.

He finally escaped from this woman and made his way to the home of his taxi driver friend. The latter was then working at night only, so he spent the day with Mike, buying him a good lunch and a few drinks. He said afterward that Mike seemed dazed, a condition which he thought at the time came from excessive drinking, but which may have been produced by dope. By evening Mike was feeling better, and the chauffeur, though he did not want to leave Mike, had to go to work.

As they sat at a café having an aperitif, Mike pulled from his pocket a tube containing pills, some of which he swallowed. He said they would make him feel better. Leaving Mike at the table, the taxi man told the proprietor of the café to keep an eye on him and, in a little while, to serve him a good dinner. This the *patron* promised to do. But hardly had his friend left, when Mike rose and walked to another café across the street. He ordered a cup of soup, put veronal in it, and shortly after fell asleep. At closing time the waiters tried to wake him, but it was impossible, and they thought him drunk. He was neither drunk nor dead, but in a coma. Since he had not paid for the soup, the café owner made a complaint and the police removed him to a cell at the station, where he was allowed to lie on a cement floor. Later they took him to a hospital, but, it being Sunday, the doctors were off duty and no further attention was paid to him until early Monday morning. Then it was too late. He died that same morning.

Mike had previously made one effort to commit suicide, but in this case I think he simply took an overdose of sleeping powder by mistake, or perhaps the effect was especially strong because of drugs previously given him.

I felt very sad over his death. So few people came to the funeral of this man who had been so popular, not even the American girl for whom he had given up Brett! Brett, if she reads this, will, I think, learn the details of Mike's death for the first time.

PERSONALITIES
OF THE QUARTER

The most vibrant flavor of personality and internationalism in Montparnasse probably came most insistently from those who had the least inhibitions rather than from the people with important names in art or literature. To the chance visitor who knew none of the writers and artists of note, the tempo of the Quarter was immediately set by such individuals as Kharis, the tall Hindu with his beautiful white turban, or Granowsky, the "Jewish cowboy," who wore chaps to ride his bicycle, or the American Indian who danced on nails, swallowed fire, and stuck pins into his skin in front of the Dôme until the police stopped him, or the Englishman with the Christ complex who dressed accordingly.

Others became part of the pattern merely by their continued presence, like the small Flemish woman with the black apron and basket of flowers who would suddenly whisper in your ear, *"Les femmes adorent les fleurs!"* I guess women do adore flowers and I guess men love to pay for them. During all my years in Montparnasse I cannot remember a night when this little flower seller did not make the rounds of every bar in the Quarter two or three times, repeating over and over again her one phrase. If you showed the least interest in her wares, she would ask you to buy, but she never insisted if you shook your head. The question put to everyone present, she would hurry out the door, her little feet scurrying up the street to the next place. I never knew her name, but once she told me of her husband. He had been in jail for some years, leaving her with five or six children to feed and care for. Her days were devoted to her offspring, her nights to flower-loving women and their escorts.

The best-known person in Montparnasse in its heyday was certainly Mitzy—"officially" the Duke of Mitzicus of Greece— who acted as guide and interpreter for all newly arrived English and Americans. Mitzy was a painter, though his real vocation was that of optimist. Never has the Quarter known a person so sure that fame and fortune were just around the corner!

"You know, James, I have received three offers to work in Hollywood and I can't decide which one to take," he used to say. "Anyway, I think I'll sail next week and make my decision when I get there." If, the next day, I asked about his motion picture prospects he would at firstly hardly know what I was talking about. "Oh, the movies? I dropped that. I've had a much better offer. I think I shall go to New York to join a big banking firm. I can't give you the name because it's a secret. I also have an offer from the French Line to decorate their new ship. I can't decide which to do. Which would you do if you were me?"

Of course while these offers were pending Mitzy was often hard put financially, though he was usually too proud to accept direct help. When he came to the Dingo he rarely asked for credit, but would say, "James, I have had so much to drink today! I mustn't drink this much. Just give me a glass of water. I wouldn't dare drink any more liquor." Of course he hadn't had a drink all day.

Mitzy was noted for his informal formality and good manners generally. This characteristic sometimes astonished Americans, and in particular a young painter with whom Mitzy shared not only a studio but a big double bed.

"I can't understand Mitzy," said the painter, who was in his early twenties. "After we are in bed and the light is put out, he insists on saying goodnight in the most formal manner and even shakes hands with me under the covers."

There was, too, old Mitrony, the Rumanian with a gray beard, poor as a beggar, but extremely erudite. He carried a quantity of books and papers under his arm and was never seen without them. He said he was writing a history of the Jews, though no one ever saw him write anything. At night he slept on chairs in the chauffeurs' restaurant near the Gare Montparnasse. Every week or so he would disappear and then a rumor went around that he was dead, but he always reappeared a few days later.

Finally he disappeared completely and was pronounced surely dead, but a friend tells me of having seen him in Bucharest not so long ago, looking much the same as ever. Old Mitrony spoke ten languages fluently and I sometimes called him in to interpret for me.

Of course Mitrony was not a "popular" figure, but still he had his influence in his quiet way, as did also the very stout Danish couple, known as "the Sun and the Moon," who sat for hours on the terrace of the Dôme drinking large quantities of liquor but rarely mixing with the crowd.

Not all were so quiet. Certainly not Francis Musgrave, or Muzzy, as he was called, an ardent Quarterite and a distinctive one with his reddish hair and red beard. He came to Paris on a short visit from London and stayed for years, earning a very meager living by journalism. Once in a fit of depression over a girl, Muzzy slashed his wrist with a razor, inflicting deep wounds that required hospital treatment. The ligaments had been cut, with the result that Muzzy has only a restricted use of his hand and the wrist is permanently bent.

It seems unfair to pick a few and say they stood out more than others. There were so many I remember vividly, like Lena Hutchins with her strange Swiss accent and a gray streak in her hair, or George Gibbs who was the spit and image of Douglas Fairbanks and liked to be taken for him. Today the headliner would be Paul Swan, the dancer, known as the most beautiful man in the world, who thrilled some Quarterites to their toes; and tomorrow it would be the woman with the mustache and long cigarette holder. Her upper lip was a complete disguise. When she finally had the hair removed she turned out to be a beauty, much to everyone's surprise and the regret of not a few dashing males who had passed her by. She was one that Charley Jones, the great womanizer, overlooked. But then the next day Bud Fisher, the creator of Mutt and Jeff, would be the center of attraction. He made a number of unintentional but living comic strips in the Dingo on several occasions.

Or if you preferred the mysterious, you could turn to the elusive and somewhat feared Countess Monici, or Catherine, who wouldn't tell her last name, or Al brown, the ankle dancer. No one knew Al's origin, though he was probably from one of the British colonies. Certainly he had traveled all over the world. His characterization of Port Said has remained a classic: "a city of broken-down French prostitutes and warm champagne."

Joe Zelli once said that the most miraculous thing in the world was to see Al Brown crossing a street, for he would stagger, just miss a taxi, hesitate, sidestep, and always arrive safely on the other side quite unconcerned.

Al was noted for his imitations, which were excellent, particularly that of a short man dancing with a tall woman, or a drunk being thrown out of a bar.

The year before I went to work in the Dingo it had been but a small bistro, a regular workman's café, without even a name, or at least no name that anyone remembers. It was bought by Harrow, a Frenchman, who called it Le Dingo, which means "the made one" in French. With the rising influx of foreigners to Montparnasse and the prosperity of the times, Harrow redecorated it, installed a bar and an English interpreter—and waited. But business did not come quickly.

It was Flossie Martin, I think, who "found" the Dingo and made it a big success. Flossie, who knew every Englishman and American in Montparnasse, brought all her friends and within a few days the place was so crowded that there was rarely a table free at drinking hours.

Harrow, with his big mustache and goatee, was immediately christened Old Man Dingo, and his portrait still hung in the bar a couple of years. Poor Old Man Dingo! He didn't know what it was all about. He spoke not one word of English, yet ninety percent of his clients spoke no French. He was making money faster than he had ever imagined possible in his wildest fancy. Night after night he wandered among the tables, smiling at his clients, watching the cash drawer, and pinching himself now and then to make sure he wasn't dreaming.

The interpreter mentioned above was a French Canadian named Mike Mery, but he was always known as Mike the Barman.

Mike came from a good family. Before the war he had been a mechanical engineer, married to a wealthy American woman whom he loved very dearly. In 1914 he joined the Canadian forces, spending the next four years in France. When he went back he discovered his wife had left him for another man. It was a great shock, for he was still very much in love. To make matters worse, she and her new husband continued to live in the same town, and the sight of them together almost drove him crazy. He left and came to France.

Mike had now lost his ambition in life. He gave up engineering and took whatever jobs came along. One day he was introduced to Old Man Dingo, who thought he could be used as a doorman and interpreter. A splendid uniform with gold braid was ordered at once, and while it was being made, Mike was allowed to help behind the bar as assistant to the barman.

Mike liked that work; he liked to mix drinks—and to take a little glass for himself now and then. He asked so many questions about bartending that the barman was amazed. Mike even bought books on mixing cocktails and studied them in his off hours. He decided to be a barman.

When the uniform arrived, it didn't fit and had to be returned. This gave Mike several more days behind the bar. When he felt quite sure of himself, he took the barman out after closing hours, gave him a few drinks, picked a fight with him, and in the end beat him up quite thoroughly.

The next day the barman failed to show up. Harrow was lost without a barman. He told Mike to phone for another, to be sent at once.

"What's the matter with me?" asked Mike. "I know English. I know the business. Let me try." Mike got the job.

And not only was he a barman, but he was one of the most

successful I have ever known. Almost from the first day, he took the limelight in the Anglo-American colony. Everyone liked his personality, and today you still hear people speak of "the good old days when Mike was barman." Friends meeting on the street would say, "Come on over to the Dingo and see Mike mix cocktails."

Of course Old Man Dingo was delighted to see his clients so pleased with his barman, and he gave Mike a free hand. People were always buying Mike drinks, inviting him to parties, taking him for automobile trips to the country, and playing up to him in every possible way.

Soon, though, Mike began to lose his hand. He began to drink too much even for his fine capacity. Breakfast for him was six Pernods, one after the other (about three lay me out), and he would continue drinking all day long. When cocktails were ordered, he would mix too much and throw the extra amount into a large bottle for himself. At the end of the evening he would drink the whole mess, shuddering as it went down. In between times he polished off a bottle of whisky!

Old Man Dingo noticed this, finally, and tried to keep an eye on Mike; but it was little use. Under the bar Mike would place a large glass of brandy or whisky, and beside it a glass of water. When Old Man Dingo was not looking, Mike would gulp the brandy, but when the boss turned around, he saw only the glass of water in Mike's hand.

Mike thought up ten different tricks for shortchanging his customers—"my ten great inventions," he called them. Most of them consisted of taking the client's money and then distracting his attention in the hope that he would walk out without asking for his change. He told his best friends of these tricks and they thought it a fine joke. Even the people who lost their money didn't mind, usually, because they liked Mike and most of them had plenty of money in those days.

I remember one trick was to take a hundred-franc note given him by a client, roll it up in a long thin strip, and place it behind his ear. Then he would do a little dance or clowning. If the customer asked for his change, Mike would say, "Your money is in sight. There it is behind my ear." He would continue his clowning, and when he felt sure the client had forgotten all about his change, Mike would make the note disappear into a drawer, amid the laughter of his friends at one end of the bar.

Mike loved to shock people without being rude to them. His favorite game was to pretend he had a girl working for him. When his girl came into the bar in the evening, he would demand money from her in a loud voice. She would say "Only fifty francs tonight, Mike," looking like a whipped cur. "Well, pass it over," he would say. Those who didn't know this was all a game would be astounded!

But Mike was too popular with his customers. They would take him away from the bar for days at a time, and then bring him back, still drunk, and push him into the Dingo. While he was away, business would drop to almost nothing. Old Man Dingo did not know what to do. He couldn't fire his popular barman and he couldn't keep him if he didn't work.

Mike had once worked at Dinard, where he had met two handsome Bretonne girls, Carmen and Arlette. He fell in love with Arlette and wanted to marry her. She told him that no such thing was possible until he had called on her parents, who lived in a big château in Brittany. Poor Mike! He hired a car one day, filled it with flowers, fruit, wine, and presents, dressed himself in his Sunday best and sped away toward the château in Brittany.

But the château turned out to be a tumbledown cottage with a string of wash hanging out in front, and inside Carmen and Arlette, much the worse for wear after drinking a bottle of brandy. Poor Mike! He loved her anyway and brought the pair to Paris. He and Arlette were to have been married as soon as he had set aside some money. Mike got the money, but in the meantime Paris had done things to the two girls. Two such attractive faces found admirers on every side. Arlette completely forgot Mike in the excitement of Paris gaiety.

Finally old Man Dingo decided to sell his bar, partly because the Anglo-Saxons made him nervous by their noise and horseplay and partly because he did not believe such a good thing could last much longer. He found a buyer in Louis Wilson, an American, and his Dutch wife, Jopie. Mike received fifteen thousand francs for arranging the deal, the money on which he planned to marry.

Mike was to continue as barman under the new management, but, what with the money he had just received and the disappointment over Arlette, he was far too drunk to appear at the opening day. Nevertheless Wilson kept him for a while, and even after he had fired him, he later gave Mike several new chances. But Mike was finished. He drank continually and never ate. He lost every job he got. Eventually he made a bum of himself, and one day became so ill he was taken to the American Hospital, where he died. Poor Mike! He had such a big chance to be a successful barman.

When I went to the Dingo Mike had been fired and Louis Smith was in charge. Louis was a very blond Englishman with a partly bald head, about which he was very sensitive, and deep bags under his eyes. He didn't last long at the Dingo because the Montparnassians thought him too distant, but he did last long enough to get himself a wife! It was like this:

Germaine was a French girl who had married an American soldier during the war. In 1922 he went back to America, but wrote regularly for many months. Suddenly his letters stopped, without explanation. Germaine wrote to his father, who replied that his son went to work as a railroad engineer one morning and never returned. Nor was he ever found.

And so, one night in 1924, Germaine happened into the Dingo. Louis asked her why she looked so downcast.

"I have been looking in a shop window, and I saw some beautiful shoes. I wish I could buy them, but I have no money."

"All right," said Louis, "here's a go. I'll shake dice with you, and if I lose, you get the shoes, but if you lose you come home with me."

Germaine lost the dice, but she got the shoes anyway! She and Louis stayed together for eight years.

After Louis we had an American sailor named Rip as barman. He was popular, but couldn't handle the crowd, so in desperation

Wilson took Mike back again. Mike didn't drink for a month, and things were fine, but it couldn't last. When he disappeared for a few days, several clients suggested to Wilson that he put me in charge, and that is how I came to be a full-fledged barman.

And now I must tell you a saga of Montparnasse. This tale begins in Rumania, where a young woman with big, dark eyes and swarthy skin decided that life was more than a gypsy camp. With a fine instinct for such things, she started a long trek to Montparnasse, earning her way as she went, selling the only thing she could. Perhaps she was beautiful in those days. When I met her in 1924 she was not.

But along the way she had acquired a daughter, or rather two, friendly little girls with a tendency to be pretty. These two she brought to Montparnasse. One we shall disguise under the name of Marie, because she is now married to a New Yorker.

But the hero of this piece—or villain, if you prefer—was a man now prominent in magazine circles in New York. We shall call him John for the sake of his present wife.

John was the ace of all spongers and credit-runner-uppers that ever hit Montparnasse, but he was different from most of the others in that he had a fine talent from which he could have made a great deal of money had he been willing to exercise it. Occasionally he had money of his own and spent it on lavish parties for his friends. When he was broke he always found a way of continuing the parties on someone else's funds. This was not hard to do, for money was plentiful and John had a winning smile and a warm personality. To his charm was added both wit and good taste.

It was in the bar of the Rotonde that John first met Marie—a case of love at first sight for both of them. Marie, who was with her mother, was poorly dressed and ill cared for, but John quickly perceived what she *might* be if she were properly fixed up. He also saw how to handle the mother.

"I want your daughter," he said to the old woman. "How much—"

"Three hundred francs a month," said the old woman, her eyes glistening, "for the first year, two hundred francs a month for the second year, and one hundred francs a month for the third year, and after that she is yours."

"Is it usual to buy the girls on the installment plan in your country?"

"Yes, sir. That is the custom of Rumania. I am Rumanian. I cannot go against my own customs."

"Well, old lady," said John, "in America we have other customs. But I am generous. We will compromise."

"Sir," said the old woman, "two hundred francs a month for one year only is my last price, but I must have four hundred of it at once."

"You are a sensible woman," said John. "Here is two hundred, and I will give you another installment next month."

John then took this small, frightened, fifteen-year-old girl to his apartment on the Champs Élysées, and it is reported that he at once gave her a thorough bath, probably her first experience in a real hot-and-cold-water tub. When the dirt was removed, John saw that Marie was beautiful, that she was bright and might be charming, that she was all that he had hoped for, that she was really worth two hundred francs a month.

From that day forward John devoted himself to Marie, and the result was certainly a credit to his artistic ability. He taught her to speak English with a charming French accent; he taught her to play the piano; he taught her to sing; he taught her to wear clothes, and bought her the very best that the great dressmakers of Paris could offer; he taught her charm of manner; and he taught her many other fine things. After a year Marie was one of the most charming and best-dressed women in Paris, a girl that anyone would be proud to know.

When Cézanne painted a picture, he looked at it for a moment, put it aside, and promptly forgot it forever. And so with John. He had created Marie, and as soon as she was "finished" he lost interest. But a woman cannot be set aside so easily. Marie was passionately in love with John. He had created her as a woman and she was not going to lose her personality as soon as she had found it.

And so began a struggle between John and Marie that occupied the attention of Montparnasse for a long time. Sympathies were with Marie, of course, for in the end John took to brutalizing her. Her mother brutalized her too, for the balance of the money had never been paid, and the mother tried to induce her daughter to leave him. But she wouldn't. She preferred to be beaten by both John and her mother.

It is a curious fact that as soon as the guiding hand of John was removed, Marie showed no taste whatsoever in clothes. She wore the same dresses, but managed to twist them so that they hung badly, or she combined the wrong colors, yet her poise and charm of manner remained.

Then one day, without warning, John returned to America, leaving Marie to struggle along as best she could. But he had given her a profession, for singing and playing in cabarets provided her with a good income for several years.

Marie continued to love John and even went to New York to see him, but all was over. Today Marie is married to another American with whom she is, I believe, very happy, and her sister is married to a prominent Englishman.

Two persons who are always associated in my mind because I saw them together frequently are Isadora Duncan and Bob Chanler, the American painter. So much has been written about the great dancer that I shall only add here what is of my personal knowledge, or what I believe has not been printed elsewhere.

I saw her first, for a short time, in 1923 while working at the Crillon, and would not have remembered her but for the fact that her young Russian husband, Sergei Essenine, caused so much trouble in the hotel that he was finally put out. Essenine was a tall, blond man with eyes that were slightly mad—at least they were mad when he was drunk, and I never saw him in any other condition. He was like a naughty boy, a big spoiled child.

In 1927, when I was at the Parnasse bar, Isadora Duncan, who was divorced from Essenine by then, took a studio in the building above, and as long as she stayed there I saw her practically every day. She was what I call a good drinker. That is, she did not seem to limit herself, yet she never took too much, and the drinks never seemed to have any effect upon her except to make her gay. I remember her blue eyes were always steady, always a little amused. She was very nice to me.

"You are a nice boy, Jimmie," she would say.

She gave frequent parties in her apartment upstairs and I was sometimes called to serve, and once she and Bob Chanler gave a big party in the bar for a group of writers and painters. It was a very gay affair and lasted right through the night.

At one time she announced her engagement to Bob Chanler in the hope that the resulting publicity would help the sale of her book. I think Isadora Duncan must have been a bit vague about it all, as part of the time she seemed to live in a dream from which she could not wake. A newspaper reporter found her in my bar and asked her if the report of the engagement were true.

"Well, I can't say yes and I can't say no," she replied.

"And what are your plans, Miss Duncan?"

"Plans? Oh, yes. Why, engaged or not, we are going to Barbades! Very soon!"

"Barbades? You must mean Barbados!"

"No, I don't. It is Barbades. I don't know just where it is or what it is, but it is somewhere on Bob's estate!"

Although Isadora Duncan felt she had lost many of her friends and that she was being persecuted for her communist beliefs, I know there was great affection for her among the people of Montparnasse and everyone was very much shocked when she died. Two faithful friends were Alan Ross MacDougal, her secretary and biographer, and Captain Patterson.

Patterson is a distant relative of both Pat Guthrie and Lady Duff Twysden, and is said to be a descendant of a king of Scotland. He is now married to the Countess Monici, who is also a familiar figure in the Quarter. Though he has only one leg, it was Captain Patterson who rescued Isadora Duncan when she walked into the sea one night on the Riviera with the intention of committing suicide.

Raymond Duncan, Isadora's brother, has long been a resident of Paris and is often seen in the Quarter, though I have never heard of his visiting a bar. He and his pupils were conspicuous figures in their flowing Grecian robes and open sandals. But unlike Isadora, Raymond's talents were combined with a good commercial sense, someone having called him "the Greek-robed member of the Chamber of Commerce." Many will remember St. Granier's famous line as he skipped across the stage of the Casino, "*N'est-ce pas que j'ai l'air Duncan?*"

Bob Chanler was a far more familiar figure in Montparnasse than either of the Duncans. Despite his wealth and success as a painter, he remained at heart a true bohemian, and the stories of his eccentricities are innumerable. Bob liked to drink with good company around him and there were periods when he was in my bar every day.

Bob was one of four brothers, all of whom were famous in one way or another. William Astor Chanler, the oldest brother, was a hero of the Spanish-American War, a congressman, a writer of popular novels about Central America, the owner of a successful racing stable, and an African big-game hunter of note. Another brother, Lewis Stuyvesant Chanler, was formerly lieutenant governor of New York and a leader of Bahaism, an Eastern philosophy, in the United States.

A third brother was John Armstrong Chanler who ran amuck, shot his butler, and effected a sensational escape from Bloomingdale Asylum in New York to Virginia, where he was judged legally sane and continued to live.

In the meantime, Bob, who was divorced from his first wife, Julia Chamberlain, had become involved in matrimony with Lina Cavalieri, celebrated European music-hall beauty. Bob told me she had married him for his money and had absolutely refused to have anything to do with him after their marriage. "She wouldn't even let me come in the bathroom when she was taking a bath," he said.

And so they separated following a big scandal and much publicity. Lina Cavalieri asked huge alimony and demanded the right to divorce him.

In the middle of all this rumpus, when Bob was beside himself and with the bother, fuss, and fighting of the case, when the papers carried daily columns about it, there arrived from this brother in America the following cable which has become famous:

WHO'S LOONEY NOW

Another famous story about Bob concerns an evening he invited Andrew Dasberg to his house for a convivial party. After dinner Bob showed his friend through the elaborate rooms.

"Well, Andy, how do you like this house?" he said. "And how do you like this room? This room is my favorite."

"It's fine, Bob, fine. However—you don't mind my being frank with you, do you?—I really think this room would be better if this door and wall were removed, making the two rooms into one."

"Perhaps you're right, Andy. Yes, I think you're right. Suppose we fix it right now."

In the cellar they found some tools, left overnight by workmen. Taking them upstairs they proceeded to tear down the offending door and wall. It was hard work and it took them several hours, but when they had finished they were thoroughly pleased. Of course at the same time they had so thoroughly wrecked both rooms that they had to be almost entirely rebuilt!

Once Bob was asked by the wife of the American ambassador to decorate a small circular room at the embassy.

When Bob answered the summons the ambassador's wife showed him the room.

"It's a fine room, don't you think, Mr. Chanler?" she said.

"Yes," he said, "a fine room."

"And our committee would like you to decorate it, Mr. Chanler. We think it would be a fine monument to you."

"Yes, so do I," was the response.

"And how much would you charge, Mr. Chanler, to do this work?"

"Twenty thousand dollars." There was no hesitancy in his response. The ambassador's wife was a bit taken back.

"Why . . . well . . . I'll have to submit that to the committee, Mr. Chanler. That is more than we planned to pay."

A few days later Bob again called on the lady.

"I'm very sorry, Mr. Chanler, but our committee cannot afford twenty thousand dollars, and so we have decided to marbleize the room, instead."

"That's a good idea," said Bob. "A very good idea."

"I'm glad to have your opinion, Mr. Chanler. Could you tell me of someone who could do a really good job of marbleizing?"

"I'll marbleize it."

"You will? Oh! How wonderful, Mr. Chanler! What would you charge?"

"Twenty thousand dollars."

I knew Bob best when I was at the Parnasse Bar and he lived in one of the studios upstairs. He often kept a taxi waiting in front of the door, and when I could get someone to take my place, we would make the rounds of Montmartre together, always ending the evening at a tripe shop near Les Halles at five or six in the morning. He made a striking figure with his big broad shoulders, his large black hat, and his curly gray hair, stalking from bar to bar.

The Parnasse was full of girls in those days, and Chanler knew them all. He would take them—there might be thirty—up to his studio, have them undress and line up in military formation. Then, while he sat in a chair, issuing commands, they would march back and forth across the room. When he had tired of this sport he would give them a hundred francs apiece and send them downstairs again. Maybe he had a secret desire to be a general in the army!

Bob's parties were not only expensive, but very noisy, partly because of his peculiar, high, liquid scream something like a police siren. Often a crowd would gather in the street, staring up at the window from which issued such diabolical noises.

In the end his mind was partially affected, and his daughter sent for Paul, his little Filipino boy who had always cared for him in New York. But in Paris Paul was useless, for he spoke not a word of French and he seemed to prefer the gay life himself.

One night Bob, who had a fine sense of melodrama, saw a face at the window, an evil face that was intent on harm. "Paul," he said, "Paul, do you see that face? It is gone now, but it will come back! Paul, take out your knife and I will take my revolver. See, Paul, I have my revolver. I am going to shoot. When I shoot, throw your knife at the same time—just as soon as the face comes back again." And Bob slowly raised his hand, as though holding a revolver, now pulling the trigger, now lowering his aim. But in his hand was nothing. Paul, too, used an imaginary weapon, aiming and throwing as though with a real knife.

But the face reappeared time and again despite all that Bob could do. Only in the morning, after an exhausting night for both of them, did Bob fall asleep and the imaginary defense against an imaginary face come to an end. Later that day Bob decided to take a suite at the Ritz, where he often stopped, but the taxi took him to the asylum at St. Mandé instead.

Later, cured of his mental ills, he went to America and died there. In his will he stipulated that everyone who attended his funeral must be drunk if they had any respect for his wishes. It is reported that at least some of the mourners were as drunk as Bob would have liked to see them.

The story of Bob's breaking down the wall of his house reminds me of an evening when three of us—a naval officer attached to the United States Embassy, John Mahon, an old-timer, and I—did some fancy drinking in Montparnasse. About seven o'clock in the morning we found ourselves in the Sélect where some French workmen were preparing to lay a new cement floor. We sat watching them, while the naval officer and John made comments on the awkwardness with which the workmen went about their business.

"I've laid cement," said the naval officer, "many times, and I know I can do a better job than that!"

"Me too," said John.

"What say we show them how?"

"OK."

I had not been consulted in this matter, and my enthusiasm for laying cement was not bolstered by any professional pride. Nevertheless I found myself carrying and mixing, without choice.

The workmen were at first annoyed and then amused, and finally rather impressed, I think. Certainly John and the naval officer knew what they were about. At the end of three hours we had laid the finest cement floor that had ever been laid in Montparnasse, so we said. At any rate it is still there in the Sélect today, after all these years!

Of course laying cement is not the cleanest job in the world. John and the naval officer, particularly, were sorry spectacles, splattered from head to foot with cement. To make matters worse, we had no more money.

"Such a fine floor," said the naval officer, "deserves celebration. I suggest we walk to the embassy. I will get some money and then we can drink justice to such a strong and well-laid floor."

And so we walked to the embassy on the Right Bank. "You wait here, and I'll be right back," our friend said. We waited. We waited some more. The naval officer never reappeared and we never saw him again. Whether the ambassador caught him, spanked him, and sent him home, or whether he was afraid to come back to wicked Montparnasse, we never knew. If he reads this book I wish he would write and tell me!

MY "BEST" BAR

I called the Trois et As my "best" bar because I had more fun there than in any other place I worked in Montparnasse. Those who remember it have the same impression, that it was an exceptional place while it lasted, which wasn't long. The Trois et As, which means "The Trey and the Ace," was located near the Senate and somewhat remote from the Montparnasse district, though its habitués were mostly Quarterites. It was connected with a small, dark hotel, and both were managed by Madame Camille, a very good-looking woman with snow-white hair. She had run away with a wealthy Parisian in her young days. After travels and adventures in Australia and South America they had returned to Paris, where she had become reconciled with her family, who opposed the marriage at first. Then she and her husband went to the States and lived for some time in California.

But this fine romance went on the rocks and they were divorced, Camille receiving a lump sum settlement, with which she started her ventures in hotels, nightclubs, and bars. First she purchased a hotel in the rue Cambon; then sold this to buy the Théâtre des Deux Masques in Montmartre; then she had a nightclub called Shanley's, later known as Kiley's. Madame Camille was not very successful financially, largely because of her impulsiveness, but her worst failure followed her purchase of a huge restaurant concession at the Decorative Arts Exposition of 1924. In 1927 she opened the Trois et As and I went there as barman three months later.

The Trois et As was not the madhouse of many people that most of my Montparnasse bars had been. Because of its out-of-the-way

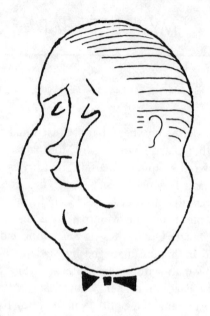

JIMMIE

from a drawing by Hilaire Hiler

position, the number of clients was few, but they were mostly good drinkers and steady customers, and they were all congenial. It was like a private club where friends would gather almost every evening, drinking until the wee small hours. I used to stand behind the bar and laugh until my sides ached at the antics of some of them.

Two stools at the bar were occupied most of the day and night by two brothers, Alsatians of good family, one of whom had a beautiful white Eskimo dog which he had brought from Labrador. Between the two, they consumed three or four bottles of port a day. They never took anything else, but port in such quantities was enough! These two were pests, at times, because I had to keep an eye on them lest they remove their trousers, a habit which seemed to have no particular cause or reason. One was a medical student and had his pockets full of instruments with which he would pretend to operate on other people. The other was a law student. At times, too, they became very insulting to foreigners, and as a result, both of them being poor fighters, they were badly beaten on several occasions. That never kept them from the bar, however.

A very popular character was Rafael Escoba, a South American who lived in the hotel upstairs and spent some fifteen thousand francs a month at the bar. We called him La Cucaracha. He had a fondness for jokes, which he would tell in a mixture of French, Spanish, and a little English. As he talked he acted the story with elaborate gestures and considerable noise.

One of the regulars was old Billy, an Englishman who had been a client in several of my bars. Billy was the delight of the girls because he spent his money on them, was attentive in the old-fashioned way, and believed everything they told him. And how Billy liked the girls! He has been attentive to literally hundreds of them in his long career. "James, she's a charming girl," he would say in reference to his love of the moment. Not that Billy was fickle. Far from it. He found the girls, brought them to the bars of Montparnasse, bought them things they wanted, and then someone else walked off with them. That happened time and again. Perhaps this accounted for Billy's prejudice against American men, whom he called "Scandinavians." Yet I think he preferred American women to English.

Billy was a writer of detective stories. He had been married twice and still paid alimony to both wives. He was no longer young, but had his own special formula for good health: in the morning, first thing, a big drink of whisky, a cold bath, another whisky, a substantial breakfast, and then to work. During the work he finished the bottle. He was always remarkably well.

We used to call him "Roast Beef" for the frequency with which he would order cold meat and bread. Once, at the Falstaff, Joe, the waiter, put his beef on a slice of bread, the bread on a paper doily, and the doily on a plate. Over the whole thing was poured a generous helping of tomato sauce. Poor Billy! He ate everything, paper and all. When he finished, he said, "James, I think there must have been paper in that sandwich!"

But to come back to the Trois et As, Billy was a constant client, often accompanied by Daphne Stone, a former show girl in England. Everything Daphne said (and her voice carried for uncalculated distances) made Billy chuckle. Their appearance—Daphne, very thin towering far above short, stout Billy—made everyone else chuckle.

And now we get down to the corrida, as it was called. A corrida is a bullfight and Rafael used the term to signify the evening's entertainment. So famous did the corrida become that people would pop in the door and ask what time it started, as though it were a paid show. The program usually started with Rafael, who did an excellent imitation of a bullfight, using a red rag which was kept behind the bar for the purpose. Even an imaginary bull had to be very small, of course, for the whole place was tiny. The crowd would form a circle, Rafael in the middle, swinging his arms, waving his "cape," and yelling at the top of his voice in Spanish.

Next, Mrs. J——, an American tourist, would do some fancy dancing with the policeman on that beat. The policeman was a favorite of hers, and when he didn't come in, the evening was spoiled. As they danced, they whirled; as they whirled, his blue cape would sail out like the skirt of a ballet dancer, while her skirt came up sufficiently to show the ends of a pair of brightly colored bloomers. Mrs. J——— always wore bloomers of violent colors, and she always displayed them (modestly, of course) before the evening was over.

Then Pat Guthrie would lay two forks on the floor and launch into the Highland fling, which he did very well. Lady Duff Twysden might be there, too, with George King, and they would do a duet at the piano. The end would come with the two Alsatian brothers who did an excellent mock trial.

Perhaps all this wouldn't have been so funny if brought right out in the daylight, but in that small bar, among friends, and in that peculiar atmosphere, it was great fun. Count Karolyi was a particular enthusiast of our corrida.

I do not know how to describe the atmosphere of the Trois et As, but whatever it was, it certainly produced drunkenness. Never have I seen so many people intoxicated, considering the comparatively few clients we had. On nights when Rafael and his harmless entertainment were missing, the clients often staged a corrida of another kind. Such fights! Particularly dangerous was Madame Camille's boyfriend, an American half her age, who landed in jail several times but was rescued by Camille after much running from *commissaire* to *commissaire*. One night an English chorus girl literally cleaned everyone out of the place. Suddenly, after several drinks, she tore off most of her clothes, and with fists clenched, started to pummel everyone present. Clad only in a pair of lace panties, she was a ridiculous sight, and we all laughed. Angered, she started throwing things, and before she was through I was hiding under the bar, Madame Camille had run upstairs, and the clients were in full flight down the rue de Tournon. When everyone was gone she came to the bar and, without seeing me, made herself another drink, sat down at a table, and gently went to sleep!

On another occasion the son of one of America's foremost

bankers came in, already at least two sheets in the wind. Without any preliminaries, he picked up a siphon bottle and squirted water in the faces of all those present. At once there was a fight, led by Mike Ward, which continued until after closing time, when I finally managed to push them all out. Mike, incidentally, is the man who came into the Dingo with seventy thousand francs in his pocket and dared anyone to take it away from him. Although Mike is not a big man, no one spoke up!

Ernest Hemingway and Mike were very close friends. One day Mike came to Hemingway. "I got in a terrible fight about you yesterday," Mike said. "I was in Harry's Bar and I heard two men talking about you. I couldn't hear what they were saying, but I kept hearing the name Ernest Hemingway. So I went over to them and I said, "Are you friends of Ernest Hemingway?' And they said, 'No.' So I socked them both!"

The Count de C———, a Frenchman with a very distinguished old name, became a steady client of ours when he discovered that Madame Camille would give him credit. The count's family had money, but he had just had a fight with his father and was living on his own, which meant us. We did not mind much, however, because he was a very likable chap who brought us as many clients as he could. Madame Camille would let him drink within reason, but she would never give him anything to eat, and he, poor man, had no money to buy food. And so, whenever he got the opportunity, the count would reach his hand into the icebox which stood in the hall. He became quite expert at this, particularly in lifting pieces of sausage. Eventually Madame Camille suspected and waited for him behind the door one evening. When he reached in as usual for the sausage, she banged him on the head with a broom handle, and from then on we always asked him if he would have any "wooden sausage" with his drink!

Aleister Crowley, the English mystic, often played chess with his friends in the bar—and always won! One of his opponents claimed that Crowley hypnotized him into losing!

Crowley and I were great friends, though he somewhat awed

me. At one time he talked of backing me in a bar of my own, but nothing ever came of it.

Although we had no license for music, we had for a long time a fine Hawaiian orchestra, composed of a Greek, his Australian wife, and a young Australian boy of whom the Greek was frequently jealous. In fact the Greek was jealous of everyone who looked at his attractive wife. She often mixed with the clients, and one night when she was dancing with a young American called Jack, her husband jumped to his feet and landed a blow square to Jack's jaw. I jumped around to separate them and was forced to lay the Greek on the floor and sit on him before he could be quieted. That episode almost broke up the orchestra!

Jack, who had a penchant for married women, got himself into a scrape on another occasion when he became entangled with a woman who lived with her husband in the hotel. One night the husband was in the bar and his wife was ill in bed upstairs. Clutching a tube of aspirin, Jack hurried to the second floor to offer them to the wife. The husband suspected nothing, but suddenly finding himself minus a handkerchief, ran upstairs to get one. On opening the door he found Jack sitting on the bed talking to the wife. It could have been passed off very easily, considering the excuse of the aspirin, but Jack had a guilty conscience and dove through the window, landing unhurt two floors below on the sidewalk. Picking himself up as fast as he could, he ran off down the street, and didn't reappear in the bar for a whole week. The husband had thought nothing of the matter, however, and when he next saw Jack they became fast friends.

A bar is a clearinghouse for complexes, but it is rarely that two persons with the same complex get together. If they could only be paired off! But it never works that way. Drinking brings out many fine and likable qualities in people, I think, but it also works havoc to many, especially women. There are so many men who become mellow with drinking, gay, or imaginative, but women so soon become hysterical, pugnacious, or, more often, highly amorous. I saw so many couples break up after a year around the bars of Montparnasse! It was not Montparnasse that did it, but drinking. At first everything was fine, but sooner or later one of the two would weaken, if they went in for excessive alcohol. Americans, especially, did not understand the meaning of moderation—a result, I suppose, of prohibition.

I know of one pair who presented a rather curious mixture of reactions. The man, Henry, came of a good family in the South of the United States and had inherited a comfortable income from his father. Work had never soiled his hands, and a previous unsuccessful marriage had left him unembittered. I first knew him in the Dingo and, later at the Trois et As, as a generous, jovial, quiet drunk. He was not in any morbid state of degeneration, but simply a man who had started drinking in his twenties and kept it up, day after day, for twenty years or more. He had had two or three mistresses who had been very fond of him and whom he had treated well. He seemed destined to go through life that way.

Then he met Helen, a woman who was no drunkard, but liked the companionship of bars. She had had a life of struggle and some success in business in New York. Henry and Helen took to each other almost at once and were happy together, living in the free and easy way of Montparnasse. Henry took a new interest in life, purchased a boat and went in for sailing on the Mediterranean, traveled more than he had previously, and, much to everyone's surprise, slackened noticeably in his drinking, though the only reason he drank less was that part of his time was now otherwise occupied. I think there is no doubt that these two were very much in love at that time.

They lived this sort of life for four years, and then, on a trip home, they were married! Whatever there is in being mumbled over by a magistrate, I don't know, but it wrought havoc to these two. Whereas previously Helen had caused Henry to drink less by providing new interests for him, now she began to demand that he stop entirely. Demand, you understand. Henry had never been commanded to do anything in his life. Helen's whole life became absorbed in the desire to have a husband who was not known as an alcoholic, or perhaps it was a passionate desire, based on pride, to reform him. Their life became one continued fight over liquor, to the point where their friends no longer cared to see them together.

The climax came one night in a bar, when she tried to have him taken by force to a sanatorium (he thought it was an insane asylum!). He was saved only by the intervention of a friend who happened to know the ambulance doctor. Henry, a wild fear in his heart, fled from Paris, going from country to country, covering his tracks as best he could. In the end they were divorced, but in the meantime his mind had become distorted from his fear of her.

If I had been more knowing in the old days I would have encouraged, and urged, some of the people who wanted to back me in a bar of my own. If I had, I might be wealthier today. One who was quite serious about it was Nancy Cunard, daughter of the shipping family. Her idea was, I think, to have a semiprivate bar, mainly for her friends, a sort of gathering place and club, and we even reached the point of discussing the Trois et As purchase price with Madame Camille. Nothing came of it, though.

Nancy Cunard was one of my faithful customers, following with her friends whenever I changed to a new bar. I have a great admiration for her fine looks and independent character.

She took a great interest in the colored race and for a long time was accompanied everywhere by a colored secretary, who was also a pianist. He used to play for us when I was at the Falstaff. Later, in New York and London, she received some very unkind publicity for her interest in the residents of Harlem.

Miss Cunard was one of the promoters of the surrealist movement in painting and writing and did much to encourage this group of artists who were then making themselves known. In this she was much aided by Louis Aragon, the writer.

When Diaghilev put on his *Ballets Russes* at the Sarah Bernhardt theater, in 1928, Max Ernst was selected to do the *décors* of a ballet based on a Spanish court story of the seventeenth century. The story tells how the ladies of the court suddenly changed their style in clothes without apparent cause and much to the astonishment of the gentlemen. The new style called for a small pillow to be sewed into the front of the dress so that each of them had a bulging stomach. However, the real reason concerned a secret of the Infanta, because in following the style she herself would have no need of a pillow!

The subject lends itself to the imagination and Ernst would have had considerable success had he not made the error of announcing himself on the posters as Max Ernst, the surrealist. The surrealists, who are, of course, ardent radicals, strongly resented his having dared to link their name with a reactionary White Russian organization such as Diaghilev's.

On the opening night the house was crowded with distinguished personages of Paris. High up in a box sat Miss Cunard with several friends, while through the audience were scattered the outraged surrealists. As the curtain rose on the Ernst *décors* hundreds of handbills, denouncing Ernst in no uncertain terms, fluttered down from the box into the audience, while from all parts of the theater came the shrill screams of police whistles, the blare of horns and even trumpets. There was pandemonium!

It didn't last long, for the *gardes républicaines* who police the theaters in Paris rushed in and soon the surrealists and their friends found themselves on the sidewalks. Nevertheless the management rang the curtain down on Max Ernst's *décors* and continued with the next number. Nancy Cunard had won her victory.

The only person who suffered unjustly in the combat was poor Constant Lambert, who wrote the music and who had done nothing to antagonize the surrealists.

Miss Cunard was often accompanied to my bar by her cousin, Victor Cunard.

"You know, James," he would say quite seriously, "I'm frightfully broke—only a hundred thousand francs in the bank!" Whereupon Miss Cunard would agree, "Yes, Victor is frightfully broke!" It must have been sad.

Miss Cunard gathered around her quite a group, most of whom were noticeable for their thinness. Nancy Cunard herself was very thin, and they said she wore bracelets so she would rattle when she walked! Mary Beerbohm, niece of Max Beerbohm, was another of the thin ones, and she too did her bit to help the surrealists.

Today the surrealists are getting a lot of notice in England and America, but Nancy Cunard is no longer a leader among them. Salvador Dali seems to be the best known now. I have seen him in Paris but he did not frequent the bars. From all reports about him he is a very serious and hard worker, keeping much to himself in his studio near the Parc de Montsouris. In the summer he goes back to his home in Catalonia where he has built a surrealist house in the middle of an olive grove.

But Marcel Duchamp and Man Ray, two more of the surrealists, were much better known around the bars. Marcel, of course, has become a legend, something out of the past, as though he were already dead. On the contrary he is very much alive, but such is his elusiveness, and such is his authority in art matters, that few ever get to know him.

Marcel Duchamp, who has been called—and rightly—the most charming man in Paris, was one of the founders of cubism. In America he was particularly known for his painting "Nude Descending a Staircase," which created a furor at the time it was first exhibited and even today produces floods of comment whenever it is shown. But after that big success Marcel committed artistic suicide because he was too much copied. I do not think he has painted a picture since, though he is now making surrealist "objects." Mostly, though, he has been expending his energies on chess, in which he is a real expert. He told me once of a huge chessboard he had in Buenos Aires which was painted on a large wall. For pieces, barbs were used, which were thrown at the wall when a new move was to be made! Sounds a bit like a story to me, but I do know that in his apartment in Paris the walls are fairly well covered with large, perpendicular chessboards on which he is constantly working out problems. The pieces are hung on little nails on the boards.

Recently I asked Marcel to tell me what he thought of Montparnasse in its heyday. He answered me in writing:

"Montparnasse was the first really international colony of artists we ever had. Because of its internationalism it was superior to

Montmartre, Greenwich Village, or Chelsea. Heretofore the essence of the art colonies had always been students, as in the Latin Quarter, but Montparnasse is dead, of course, and it may take twenty, fifty, or a hundred years to develop a new Montparnasse, and even then it is bound to take an entirely different form. The grouping of people through a common interest, as in Montparnasse, is equally true of the movie actors who have grouped themselves in Hollywood, an industrialized, popularized Montparnasse.

"I thoroughly agree with Jimmie's theory that the colorful but nonproductive characters of Montparnasse often contributed greatly to the success of the creative group. Liquor was an important factor in stimulating the exchange of ideas between artists."

Marcel is a competent judge, too, for he at one time lived in Greenwich Village (where he published *The Blindman*) and he has also lived in Chelsea, I believe.

A close friend of his is Man Ray, photographer par excellence and now maker of "objects" under the surrealist banner. It was he who "created" Kiki by taking her to all the Montparnasse parties and by encouraging her in individual self-expression. I asked Man, too, what he thought of Montparnasse, and he replied:

"I can see no reason for the continuance of the human race. The sooner it dies, the better. Montparnasse has done much to help the cause."

TOURISTS

Even in 1924 there was always a goodly number of tourists in Montparnasse. Some of them were mere curiosity seekers who came to look at "the wild artists in their den," but by far the larger number at this time were those who sought to lead the bohemian life as an exciting change from churchgoing in the Corn Belt or rural England.

The intensity with which some of these people—and especially the women—went about the business of being "artistic" was a study in itself. Many of them, really highly respected and stable citizens at home, went completely berserk the minute they hit Montparnasse.

I remember one time walking from the Dôme to the Dingo. Ten feet or so ahead of me was Flossie Martin. As she came abreast of the bar entrance, a handsome Rolls-Royce drove up to the curb and from it stepped two lavishly dressed ladies. For a moment they hesitated. They looked at the Dingo questioningly. They peered in the windows between the curtains.

Flossie, seeing them, looked her contempt. As she passed into the bar she tossed a single phrase over her shoulder:

"You bitch!"

Whereupon the lady so addressed nudged her companion anxiously.

"Come on, Helen," she said. "This must be the place!"

The tourists who stuck around were eventually absorbed into the life of Montparnasse. Usually they became fixtures at the bars, and but few of them pretended to more than "an interest" in art or literature. Some, however, really felt the necessity of making a stab at painting. This usually consisted in attending one of the croquis classes in the rue de la Grande Chaumière two or three times a week, making a dozen bad charcoal sketches each time, and from then on speaking of "Art" as though it were a secret society into which only a chosen few were initiated.

One couple who came to Montparnasse "because they were so interested in 'art'" was from Chicago. The husband had made a small fortune in the hardware business out there, then, at the age of fifty, he and his wife had suddenly turned bohemian. She decided to sing, as I recall it, while he decided to paint. Both wished to make friends with the natives, to which end they gave huge cocktail parties every Saturday afternoon. Crowds of two hundred or more went to their studio on the rue Campagne Première to drink fine brandy and whisky. No invitation was necessary. "In bohemia there is open house." The couple felt very pleased with themselves at first, but in a few weeks even they saw that their guests were only hangers-on, wandering English, Americans, and French who took whatever was free. Of real artists there were practically none.

The couple returned to America sadly disillusioned.

Then there were those who tried to patronize the arts by patronizing the artists. To this class belongs a former official of a large steamship organization, who has been patronizing Montparnasse and the Latin Quarter in the wrong way since Whistler's day. In fact, he tells everyone how he lent money to Whistler, who never returned it. The shipping magnate feels that Whistler owes everything to him!

The tourists gave rise to many fine stories. One I have always enjoyed concerns a woman who had been in Paris but a couple of days. Meeting on the street a friend off the same boat, she said, "You know, I've been here two whole days and I haven't been to the Louvre yet!"

"Well, you know," said her friend, "I haven't either. I think it must be the hard water!"

Another story, a true one, concerns a woman and her son from Chicago. She and her husband had worked hard all their lives, he with a small business, she with her housework. A few years after the war, however, the husband died, and when the will was filed, the wife was amazed to find that she had a substantial income from the business.

"I will travel," she thought. "I will take my son and I will go far away." First they went to Washington, and were duly interested. The son, then about twenty, showed great enthusiasm for this traveling.

Then they went to Florida. That seemed wonderful. Why not on to Europe? They went.

When a friend of mine met them in Italy they had been in Europe for over a year. The mother was a little, wrinkled, yet energetic and cheerful woman, while the son was tall and silent.

"My dear," said the mother, "I must admit that I am just a little tired of Europe. I hope I can persuade my son to go back to Chicago next month. You know we've been over here a year. We've done Belgium, Holland, Germany, Austria, France, Spain, and now Italy. I think that's enough, don't you?

"But, my dear, you don't know my son! He is very strange, and I don't understand him myself, half the time. He has such a liking for pictures! Not pictures in a book, but in these here galleries. My boy goes to all the museums he can find. Right here in Florence he's been to two already. I can't understand that!

"You know," she said, dropping her voice to a whisper, "ain't as though he looked at only the naked pictures, *he looks at them all!*"

"Queen Elizabeth" was the name we gave to one of the English visitors. No bar was complete without this very English and very snobbish lady, who insisted on being served six drinks at a time. Sometimes I would suggest that she take them one at a time.

"No, no, James! I must have them all at once. Otherwise I can't enjoy them." And then I would line up six glasses of champagne on the bar and she would drink them, taking a sip from each!

Queen Elizabeth—this one—was a stenographer with a very good job. I should say jobs, for she walked out of many of her firms after six or eight months, forgetting to come back. But she could always get a new position because of her remarkable facility in three languages.

Then there was "Miss Cancer," the tiny, chubby Southern girl with a passion for undressing in public. She got her nickname when a man who said he was a doctor examined her in one of the bars and announced after some investigation that she had a cancer of the left breast. The poor girl was quite scared and rushed to the American hospital where she paid twenty dollars for a very thorough examination, which showed, of course, that nothing was wrong. Later she learned that the man who had examined her was the proprietor of the bar!

One of the mysteries of the Quarter was Mrs. Lord, known far and wide as "The Pollywog," who was thought by many to be a German spy. She had been married to a British captain who was killed in the war, had a young son, and received a pension from the government. That she was a British subject I know, for I once saw her passport, but her English had just the faintest trace of a foreign accent.

Once I accused her of being a German spy, whereupon she hit me with a saucer. "Me! A German spy!" she shouted, "Me! I hate Germans! They killed my husband!" Probably she was a much-maligned person.

Later she was deported from France and was committed to a sanatorium near Brussels. I have heard that she died there.

Mrs. Cook, an American woman with a passion for bridge, was a very familiar figure in Montparnasse in the boisterous twenties. She is better known by her self-imposed pseudonym of Lady Betty. "Everyone calls me Lady Betty," she used to say when anyone called her Mrs. Cook.

Lady Betty was a woman no longer young and she aspired to the role of Mother of Montparnasse, a title that Carrie King had held for many years. There was some rivalry, I believe, but in the end Lady Betty won because Carrie King was sent to America by some of her friends. Carrie King, incidentally, had played Buttercup in the original production of *H.M.S. Pinafore*.

The story of Carrie King's operation has been told many times, but it is amusing enough to tell again. It wasn't amusing for her, I guess. She was a woman of over sixty, a newspaper writer, with good vitality, though naturally she showed her age. One day she decided to inquire about rejuvenation methods. It seemed a shame to her that she should feel so young, yet be so old.

Eventually Doctor Voronoff, the Vienna monkey-gland specialist, performed an operation that left her far younger in spirit and emotions but decidedly older in physical appearance.

Carrie King was never the same after that operation. The shape of her face changed, took on a definitely simian expression, and she repapered her room with a frieze of scampering monkeys. Doc Mahoney said he expected to see her jump to the chandelier at any moment and swing by her tail!

But Montparnasse felt sorry for her, nevertheless, and the Quarter supported her for more than a year. She has since died in America, I believe.

An incident that amused the whole Quarter, except the woman in question, concerned an American couple from New York. The wife had expressed to her husband her determination to buy a new evening gown, if not two.

"We are spending too much money already," he said, "and I forbid you to buy any more evening dresses."

But the lady, like a true, loving, and devoted wife, immediately ordered two gowns from a famous dressmaker. They arrived at the apartment, but it was a long time before she was able to wear either of them in public. For her husband had, the night before, painted on her back with iodine an unprintable French word which in English had its counterpart in four letters.

QUAT'Z'ARTS BALL

On the Right Bank the culmination of the spring season was the Grand Prix at the Longchamps racecourse, but on the Left Bank it was the Quat'Z'Arts Ball. After one of these events, depending on which side of the Seine you lived, you prepared to depart on your summer vacation. Paris, you know, has two "seasons"—spring and fall. In between time is the winter which lasts from the end of November to the end of February, short, miserably cold and damp days, when everyone who can flees to winter sports in the Alps or sunshine in North Africa. The summer, on the other hand, is a delightful season, yet the Parisians shun it in much the same way they avoid the winter. Most of them go off to the seaside, to foreign watering places, or on leisurely trips through the French provinces. One reason for the American colony's exodus from Paris in the summer was the huge influx of touring compatriots who descended on the city at this time of year. There was nothing more objectionable to an American resident (even though he might be staying but a couple of months) than an American tourist. In the big tourist years there might be a hundred thousand Americans in the city at one time. That's a lot of Americans, whichever way you look at it!

Of course, most of them stayed on the Right Bank, because the big hotels are on that side, but thousands crossed the river to have a look at the wild men in Montparnasse. Much as you might enjoy the Quarter, you didn't like to feel yourself part of a zoo. The French, too, fled from Paris in the summer for much the same reason. It was as though two hundred thousand wealthy, noisy, strangely dressed Russians were to descend suddenly on New

York. Along Fifth Avenue, Broadway, and the other centers you would hear even more Russian than English, always in a noisy, boisterous manner. At first this might be amusing, but after a week or two it would be very tiresome. You, too, would probably wish to flee the city and retire to some quiet little resort for the summer months until the main body of Russians had returned to their native land.

Of course, another reason for leaving Paris after the Quat'Z'Arts Ball was the closing of the art academies. Painters naturally wanted to go where they could work out-of-doors, very often taking their models with them. Then by September they would be eager to return to Paris to show their summer sketches to their friends and to get back to the academies.

And so the Quat'Z'Arts Ball was more than a mere party, but a real climax to the entire year. It was preceded by a series of smaller balls earlier in the spring. Each academy gave a party in April or May, to which the students were allowed to invite as many friends as they chose. Admission was charged, of course, and generally there was a goodly balance in the coffers after the ball was over. Then the proceeds from all these academy balls were turned over to the Quat'Z'Arts committee and the entire sum splurged on the final spree of the year to which all students of all the contributing academies were admitted, as well as all the models that could be found. The Quat'Z'Arts was an orgy, and no other word describes it. The price of admission in those days was fifty francs for men and twenty francs for women. Any woman could walk in, providing she had a ticket, but only bona fide art students could come in the male contingent, ticket or no ticket.

Weeks before the party the committee would announce the ordained costume of the year. In 1924 it was early Phoenician, and such was its importance that it gave rise to a style color which is probably remembered by every woman reader of this book—Phoenician red. I don't suppose there was a big dressmaker in Paris who did not have a style scout somewhere in the crowd.

For days in advance everyone was talking of plans for the Quat'Z'Arts, looking up costume reference books, buying bottles of skin dye, working on elaborate headdresses. When I say "costume" I am referring largely to what went on the head, for it was agreed that over the body the men would wear little more than a loincloth, while the women wore only short tunics which reached from breast to thigh. The rest of the body was coated with bronze-red dye, and feet were either bare or shod with light leather sandals.

The ball that year was held in the big hall of Luna Park at the Porte d'Auteuil. It started about midnight, but festivities began much earlier. The party to which I had managed to attach myself met about six o'clock in a little restaurant on the Boulevard St. Michel for drinks and dinner, some hundred and fifty of us, all in costume. It was a noisy, uproarious dinner which lasted until nine or ten, while large crowds stood on the sidewalks outside staring through the windows. Dinner over, we started up the boulevard, arms linked in a phalanx right across the street. Ahead of us and behind us were groups of police sent there to protect us should any trouble start. I say protect *us* because this party always had official sanction from the authorities. It was an established custom that for this one night in the year the students had the right to do whatever they chose short of causing extensive damage to property or bodily injury.

And so as we marched up the broad boulevard we stopped every car that came along, removed from it any girl who seemed attractive, kissed her all around, and then proceeded to the next car. The girls so addressed took it in good part, though they were probably not so pleased when they found their faces literally covered with red paint!

Of course we were headed for the Dôme, and after galloping through it we proceeded to visit other cafés in the neighborhood. I do not remember just how I got there, but after a while I found myself on the subway with fifty or so companions, whooping and yelling and causing no end of commotion. The next thing I knew we were marching up the Champs Élysées, still kissing what attractive girls we saw, and generally raising Cain. Then someone had the bright idea of going into Claridge's Hotel, one of the large, expensive establishments in Paris, and what a time we had there!! The hotel was in a pandemonium as, half-naked, you must remember, we went screaming through the corridors, into the dining room, pulling the noses of the guests, snatching up their drinks, interrupting the dancing, even rushing upstairs to the bedrooms to open whatever doors were not locked and gaze upon the occupants in various states of dress or undress! You might think the hotel management would have objected, but they didn't, first because it was an accepted custom (and custom goes a long way in France), but perhaps more because we were backed up by a strong cordon of police. True, some of the hotel guests objected—especially some that we found in the upstairs rooms—but it all happened so quickly that we were gone before they had time to rise to any heights of indignation.

Back on the Champs Élysées, we streamed up the avenue, stopping here and there to snatch up a drink off a café table, followed by our faithful police and an ever-increasing mob of people. I do not remember just how we finally reached Luna Park, but I think we took the subway again.

At the entrance to the hall were two doors, one for women, where two committee members examined their costumes to see that they were properly (or improperly) within the category of early Phoenician, and took their tickets. At the other door, though, were eight or ten more committee members, including a couple of husky bouncers, whose job it was to weed the sheep from the goats. Of course, I was not an art student and therefore had no real right to go to the Quat'Z'Arts, but I had been carefully coached in advance by one of my art-student friends on what to say to the examiners. The first man took my ticket; the second man asked me what academy I belonged to.

"Julien Academy," I replied. He passed me on to the next man, who asked me what I studied and the name of my professor.

"Sculpture," I answered, naming a professor at the academy. With that, another man gave me a tremendous shove and I found myself on the dance floor of Luna Park. It was pretty easy, it seemed to me, yet there were plenty who did not get in. If they tried to fight their way in, the bouncers would grab them, and if they still resisted they were turned over to the police, who whisked them off to a sort of impromptu concentration camp for nonstudents where they were eventually released on their promise to go straight home.

Inside the huge hall was a sight hard to describe! There must have been two thousand men and girls in that enormous room. Some still retained their costumes, a few had abandoned them entirely, and before the evening was over most of those present were completely naked except for the red paint. That this state of nudity was prearranged was proved by the fact that the red paint had been applied to all parts of the body, and not merely to the skin left exposed by loin cloth or tunic. The crowd was largely French, of course—students and models. No Frenchwoman with the faintest shred of self-respect would even dream of attending such a ball. Not so the English and American girls, however, who represented a fair-sized minority of those present. They were not models, of course, but the daughters of highly respectable parents, and in some cases of distinctly prominent families. But this was Paris and they were out for the wildest the city had to offer. The only difference between them and the models was that our girls did not discard their tunics as the evening progressed—their only sop to homegrown morality. Many of the men, however, were not so modest.

The first event of the evening was a parade around the room, passing in front of the judges who were to award prizes for the most artistic headdresses. In this the crowd assisted, clapping to indicate their approval of the different costumes as they were paraded across a small stage at one end of the hall. That over, the crowd settled down to serious dancing, drinking, and lovemaking. Two orchestras played and the crowd danced, while from a series of small and secluded balconies others threw streamers and confetti down upon the dancers. I cannot go into details as to some of the things that happened that evening, especially in the balconies, and unfortunately they cannot safely be left to the imagination of my readers, because the normal imagination is inadequate!

I forgot to mention earlier that there was another kind of ticket to the Quat'Z'Arts which would admit the bearer without examination at the door. These were called "committee tickets" and were supposed to be given to artists of renown whose presence would lend importance to the ball. However, it was possible to buy these tickets, if one knew a committee member, for a substantial sum. Somehow an American couple, living at the Crillon Hotel, one of Paris's swankiest, had managed to obtain committee tickets to this ball of which they had heard even back home in the Middle West. So on this particular night they put on regulation evening dress and arrived by taxi at the ball at about two o'clock. Showing their tickets, they were admitted without question, but when they came onto the dance floor and the crowd got a good look at their clothes, they were immediately surrounded by a howling mob. The man and woman were in their fifties, both of them rather stout, and the wife was lavishly dressed. With whoops of glee the students dragged them into the middle of the hall and carefully disrobed them both, garment by garment! Soon they were completely naked, their clothes carried off to parts unknown. Finally they were released. Scared to death, no doubt, they made a flying leap for the door and escape. On the street and entirely naked, in front of a large crowd of curious, they obtained a taxi and returned to the Crillon, where the doorman obligingly lent them raincoats in which they fled through the lobby to their rooms. Their clothes, money, and jewelry they never recovered, for early the next morning they left Paris, probably never to return!

Others who came on committee tickets, however, were more knowing and wore appropriate costumes. They included, besides several eminent artists, two of Hollywood's most famous stars of the silent days, one of whom, despite her Mack Sennett background, had acquired high social standing.

And so the drinking and dancing continued through the night, though ranks were slowly thinned out as various inebriates and others were overtaken by a longing for sleep. Meantime, outside,

An evening at the Dingo. Jimmie Charters (left) mixes drinks, 1924.

Jimmie Charters (left), and Paris *Tribune* reporter Leigh Hoffman (far right), Paris circa 1928.

Le Dôme and La Coupole in Montparnasse, mid-twenties.

On the Dôme terrace, Paris, 1925.

Quat-z-Arts Ball, an annual celebration of art students, 1922.

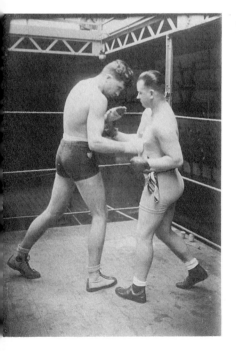

Jimmie Charters and sparring partner.

From left to right: Wambly Bald, George Antheil, and Hilaire Hiler, Paris, 1927.

A Montparnasse bar decorated by Hilaire Hiler, Paris, 1929.

Stage designer Gordon Craig and Isadora Duncan, the day they met in Berlin, 1904. *(Billy Rose Theatre Collection, The New York Public Library at Lincoln Center, Astor, Lenox and Tilden Foundations.)*

Outside the Jockey Club in Montparnasse. The back row from left to right: Man Ray, Hilaire Hiler, the "Jockey," Ezra Pound, two unidentified gentlemen, Curtis Moffat; and seated from left to right: Tristan Tzara and Jean Cocteau, circa 1930.

A portrait of Kiki from her *Memoirs,* Black Manikin Press, Paris, 1930.

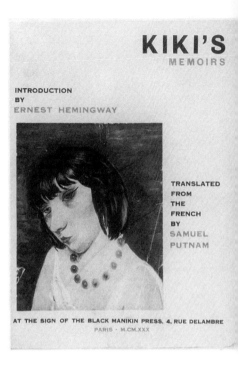

Kiki, Paris, 1924.

Portrait of Ford Madox Ford by Stella Bowen, late twenties.

Nancy Cunard, Paris, mid-twenties. *(Curtis Moffat)*

Lady Duff Twysden, the inspiration for Lady Brett Ashley in *The Sun Also Rises,* in her passport photo of 1929.

Patrick Guthrie, the inspiration for Mike Campbell in *The Sun Also Rises.*

Ernest Hemingway, early twenties.

the police were having their difficulties, with a large crowd of communists who had gathered to demonstrate against the ball. The argument of the radicals was that the ball represented special and licentious privilege for a special class (students), and consequently was contrary to communist doctrines. They attacked several of the early leavers with sticks and stones, and one American girl was slightly injured, but the police, who were there in battalions, finally dispersed the mob, and by the time the party ended the surrounding streets were almost entirely deserted.

When the orchestra finally played its last piece, there were only two or three hundred of us left, and most of us considerably the worse for wear. But we were still moving, and slowly the entire crowd straggled up the avenue toward the Place de la Concorde as the first blue lights of dawn were breaking. It is one of the customs of the Quat'Z'Arts that those who survive the night shall bathe in the fountains of the Concorde and there endeavor to wash off the paint with which they are covered. It is quite a sight to see several hundred nude bathers of both sexes splashing in the bubbling waters of that famous square. It is more a custom than an effectual bath, however, as it takes more than water to rid one of that infernal paint. It took me a good two weeks before I finally got it out of my ears and hair!

STRANGE SUICIDES

Along with the intense gaiety of Montparnasse there was bound to be a certain amount of intense melancholy, and that there were occasional suicides is not surprising. I am surprised there weren't more. So many took their emotions very seriously, at least for the moment. I have seen men and women sit at the bar and talk for hours about their troubles, and of how suicide was the only way out. But next day the same person might be back again, gay as a meadowlark.

I got so that I never believed any of these threats of suicide, so that when someone actually did kill himself, it came as a great shock. It didn't happen often, however. Most of the people who died in Montparnasse were acute alcoholics and, after all, they would have passed on from the same cause wherever they might have been.

Among the suicides, however, a few stand out vividly in my mind. There was Rita, for instance, a French girl who frequented the Anglo-American colony for several years and was very much liked by many. Rita, who had a very true and generous nature, was in love with an Argentine. When she found that he wished to leave her, she was desperate, and became temporarily unbalanced. With considerable cunning, she persuaded him to come to her room in a local hotel. Hardly had he entered when she pulled a gun from her bag and fired at him. The Argentine, with rare presence of mind, dodged the bullet and dropped to the floor as though instantly killed. For a few long seconds Rita stood there, while the Argentine lay trembling and wondering if she would fire again. Instead, she put a bullet into her own head and died almost at once. Some blamed the Argentine for not attempting to prevent her suicide, but had he moved he would probably have been killed. As it was he was held for her murder for some time, until suicide was definitely proved.

One of the strangest deaths of Montparnasse was that of Larry Murphy, a quiet and very likable American boy. He had talent as a painter and musician, money to live on, and many good friends. If anyone knows the reason he killed himself, the story has never been told.

He came to the Parnasse Bar one night after a quiet party on the terrace of the Sélect with some friends. There were few people in the bar at the time and I talked with him for half an hour. He seemed depressed, which was not usual with him, and I tried to cheer him up. He had a strange look in his eyes that I cannot describe.

"I need a strong drink, Jimmie," he said, "give me a very strong gin fizz. Perhaps that will make me feel better." I served him six, one after the other. The doorman put him in a taxi and sent him home. By that time he was rather drunk, and still depressed.

The next day we were shocked to learn that he had turned on the gas in his studio and had slowly suffocated while playing the piano. His death was a great surprise to the Quarter, and especially to several of his close friends who were much affected.

The only other time I have seen that same look in a man's eyes was one afternoon in another bar, when George Faverhill came in.

"Jimmie," he said, "I don't care what you give me, but I must get drunk right away. I have a need to be drunk, and as fast as possible." This was an unusual request, as George was not a heavy drinker in any way and was always very quiet. I mixed him several cocktails, not suspecting what was behind the request.

"I think you're all right now, sir," I said. "Don't you think you've had enough?"

"Yes, Jimmie, I've had enough. I think I'll go home." He walked out the door and up the street, but he had hardly turned the corner before he dropped dead! It was not the alcohol that killed him, but some great mental strain which the alcohol had not relieved, and had probably exaggerated. I felt very miserable about this for a long time, as it seemed in some way that I had been responsible. Yet if I had refused to serve him he would have gone to some other bar.

Another case was of two clients who were painters, two young men who were constantly together, very quiet but seemingly happy. One night I served them as usual and they did not appear upset in any way. But they did not show up again after that and friends began to make inquiries.

They had a studio on the rue Vercingétorix where they lived in very modest fashion. The *concierge* of the building became worried when she did not see them during the following week or two, and eventually was persuaded to climb onto the roof of an adjacent building and look through the studio skylight.

A fantastic sight met her gaze. On either side of a table sat the two men with a large bowl of reddish water between them. When the studio was entered it was found that they had cut their wrists, placed them in the water so that the blood would not clot, and died of loss of blood! The only motive found was that they were almost penniless, though in the meantime a letter had arrived with money.

One of the most dramatic suicides of Montparnasse, because it was in public, was that of a young California boy whose name I cannot remember. We will call him Jim. He was a painter and had long occupied a studio on the rue d'Assas. Among his friends he was known as a rather quiet chap, somewhat erratic, and always hard-pressed for money. Many wondered how he made both ends meet, for he received but a small allowance from his wealthy parents.

Jim first came into prominence when an American woman living in a Champs Élysées hotel jumped out of her window, killing herself instantly. There was no apparent reason for her suicide, particularly as she left behind a young daughter to whom she was devoted. The Paris papers speculated on the case for several days until Jim suddenly announced that he could furnish the answer to the problem. "Mrs. R———," he said, "came to see me some months ago through a mutual friend. She wished me to do a portrait and offered me a substantial sum. I consented and started to work. For a few sessions she posed in normal fashion, but then, taken with a violent passion, she made so many advances to me that I was unable to accomplish anything on the portrait. Finally, a few weeks ago, I told her that I could not go on with the canvas and that I did not wish to see her again. And that is the cause of her suicide."

At first Jim was believed, though everyone deplored his taste in telling such a personal story. Later it was seen that many of the details of his account varied with different tellings. Nor could he produce the painting he had begun of Mrs. R———. He had destroyed it, he said.

Not more than a week later, however, he was dispossessed from his studio for nonpayment of rent, and found himself actually on the street, penniless. Because of his revelations about Mrs. R——— very few made any effort whatsoever to help him.

During the week that followed his expulsion from his studio, Jim sat in the Dôme continually, day and night. He ate nothing, and he drank only white wine. His face was thin, drawn, and pale. Much of the time he spent either staring at the wall or the floor, or with his face buried in his hands. I saw many persons try to get him to eat, offer to take him home and put him to bed, but he stubbornly refused all help. He would accept only money, and with the money he bought more white wine.

For seven days we watched this man go insane, day by day getting worse. Of course we should have done something about him; we should have called a doctor; we should have had him removed. But we didn't. We didn't know that he was losing his mind.

On the seventh day I was sitting with some friends in the back room of the Dôme. Jim, who sat at a neighboring table, was more agitated than he had been. He talked to us a little wildly, in meaningless or at least incomprehensible words. Suddenly he jumped from his chair and rushed out of the room, his eyes afire. His whole appearance was indeed startling, for during the week he had been in the Dôme he had neither shaved, changed his clothes, nor washed!

On the terrace he stopped, went through some strange gestures, and was last seen running madly down the Boulevard Raspail as fast as he could go. Later that night he was picked up by the police, quite out of his head, and taken to an asylum. When his pockets were searched, a fifty-franc note was found, money that he had borrowed from an American woman on the Dôme terrace just before rushing away.

When questioned, Jim denied that he was an American citizen, managed to tear up his passport when he was confronted with it, and swore that he was of French parentage. And this seems to have been the key to the cause of his insanity. A perfectly normal boy at first, he had come to Paris to study painting and had found the life very much to his taste. However, after he had been there a year or so, his parents thought it was time for him to return to California. He refused, and used for living expenses the passage money they sent him. Eventually they cut off his allowance entirely. Still he was determined to stay. But the situation preyed on his mind. He suspected everyone of trying to force him back to America. He became insane.

Just what relations he had with his family I do not know, except that when he was committed to an insane asylum they refused to have anything further to do with him, or to bother about him in any way.

Some months later he was released from the asylum, but he lived only a short time, ending his unhappiness in suicide.

In the flourishing days of the Jockey, a familiar pair were Joe Goodman, the songwriter, author of "Rose of Washington Square" and "Second-Hand Rose," and his lawyer, Finnety. Goodman could not survive more than a few minutes without his lawyer. It was a joke in the Quarter to try to separate Joe from Finnety. They both lived at the Hotel Lutetia. Joe spoke not a word of French, yet, when he was out somewhere, he could use a telephone to reach Finnety at the hotel with great ease. Joe would pick up the receiver and when the girl answered he would say, "Cigar carrot cat carrot wheat." The number of the hotel was *Sègur quarante-quatre quarante-huit*. He always got the number without difficulty.

Poor Finnety contracted a very rare disease in which the bones of the body became slowly larger and thicker. Doctors could not cure it and Finnety was terribly depressed. He said he could not bear to look at himself in the mirror. One day Hiler heard moans in the washroom of the Jockey, and, pulling Finnety out, applied a stomach pump with great speed to extract the poison which the latter had swallowed. When he had recovered sufficiently, Hiler questioned him.

"Hiler, I cannot, I really cannot go on living. I cannot bear to see my face change. You saved me this time, but I'll do it again, and right away, too."

"What," said Hiler, "have you got against me?"

"Nothing, old man," said Finnety. "You're a fine guy."

"Then why do you want to hurt my business in the Jockey?"

"I don't, old man, really I don't."

"Well," continued Hiler, "the next time you want to commit suicide, go somewhere else. Don't come here."

"Where shall I go then?"

"Well," said Hiler thoughtfully, "the Dôme is my big rival, you know." The next day Finnety was found dead in the washroom of the Dôme.

Of course by now you have come to the conclusion that Montparnasse was nothing more than a band of drunks. But though the drinking was excessive—I couldn't deny it—there were always many serious workers among us. The renown of Montparnasse came, not from its drinking, but from its success as an artist's colony.

Montparnasse existed long before I came to it. It reached its height in 1925, and its decline in 1929. When I went to the Dingo in 1924, it was in full swing, but behind it was a colorful background of reputations and legends.

Many books have been written about the painters and writers of Montparnasse and of the Latin Quarter which preceded it as an art colony, to say nothing of Montmartre. The Latin Quarter and Montmartre have been artistically dead for a long time, and Montparnasse has now joined them, but each left its legends of *la vie de Bohême*. These tales were undoubtedly an inspiration to many a young artist.

To many English and Americans, Paris has meant women's fashions, and Oscar Wilde. About style in clothes I know nothing, but of Oscar Wilde I heard many stories, especially from Frank Harris, who was one of my clients. Frank Harris discussed Oscar Wilde with everyone. He even discussed him with me when no one else was around.

I remember particularly a story about Wilde and a famous French poetess whose name I have forgotten. Harris and Wilde were crossing the Pont Neuf one afternoon when they saw the poetess coming toward them. Harris was a bit embarrassed at presenting Wilde, for the poetess had the reputation of being the ugliest woman in Paris, and Wilde did not appreciate ugliness.

However, there was no avoiding it.

"I have heard of you," she said when Wilde was presented.

"And I of you, Madame," he replied.

"I have no doubt," she said bitterly, "I am known for my face—the ugliest in Paris." Wilde made a gallant gesture and a bow.

"In the world, Madame!" he replied.

And this reminds me of a story of Tristan Bernard, the celebrated French wit, who sometimes visited one of my bars with a group of friends.

The story concerns a bus in the days when women wore large hats and sharp hatpins. A woman thus accoutered was standing on the back platform. Next to her stood a man. At a sudden lurch of the bus she was thrown against the man and her head bent forward in such a way that he received the full effect of the hatpin in his cheek.

"*Chameau!*" he said in anger to the woman, holding his hand to his face. Now you must understand that *chameau* is a very bad word in French. Literally it means "camel," but as an expletive it corresponds to "damn you!" or worse.

The woman was very indignant. At the next stop she called a policeman and the man was arrested.

When brought before the magistrate, the man—perhaps it was Tristan Bernard himself—was asked for an explanation of his conduct.

"Do you known, Monsieur," said the judge, "that it is grossly impolite to call a lady a camel?"

"I know that," said the man. "It is true. But I would like to ask Your Honor a question."

"Certainly," said the judge.

"If it is impolite to call a lady 'camel,' is it also impolite to call a camel 'madame'?"

"Certainly not, Monsieur. I do not know why you ask such a

question. You can rest assured that you may call a camel 'madame' or anything else you choose. What has that to do with the case?"

Whereupon the man turned to the lady who had him arrested, and with a sweep of his hand, he bowed low before her.

"Madame!" he said.

I have heard other stories of Oscar Wilde but unfortunately I have forgotten them. To me Wilde was a sort of myth, like Whistler, that people talked about, until I met his niece, Dolly Wilde, with her pale face and big gray eyes.

Incidentally, Hilaire Hiler, the American painter, is said to look very much like Oscar Wilde. He hasn't the same characteristics, though.

Besides his stories of Wilde, Harris often told of Rémy de Gourmont, of how he came to Montparnasse with his face covered with a veil to hide a skin disease, never taking it off as long as others were present.

An important person in the legends of Montparnasse was old Italian Rosalie, who ran a restaurant on the rue Campagne Première until her death in 1933. Rosalie had been a model for Whistler in her young days, and so great an impression had he made on her that when her son was born, his resemblance to the painter was very marked. The son is still in Montparnasse, I believe, but he has never taken up painting.

Rosalie was the friend of many of the well-known painters, especially after she started her restaurant. Many of them gave her their paintings in exchange for food, notably Modigliani. After Modigliani's death a dealer offered to buy any drawings of his that she might have. That Modigliani's work had a value was a surprise to Rosalie, so she hurried to the cellar where she had placed a large bundle of his drawings and paintings. Unfortunately for herself, the rats had so eaten and scratched them that little remained.

Rosalie always said her restaurant was for poor artists, and on many occasions she drove from her door well-dressed visitors who came to see the artist in his lair. She would be particularly enraged by women in fur coats.

"Fur coats are for the restaurants on the Champs Élysées," she would scream at them. "This restaurant is for poor people. Good food for poor artists. Go away, rich people. You can't eat in my restaurant."

But later she changed her mind. When the crash came in 1929 they told her of the rich people who no longer had any money, and she became sorry for them. Thereafter she welcomed the fur-coated gentry, saying, "They are used to fine things, but now they have no money!"

And yet Rosalie was a canny businesswoman. She sold her restaurant to two American women some years ago for a handsome price, and then, when trade fell away (the restaurant was nothing without Rosalie's big smile), she bought it back for a song and built up the clientele again in a few weeks. I believe she did this a second time, later, with a French couple. Rosalie's meals were quite good and very cheap, but she had little expense beside the food, for the tables were plain marble with wooden benches, and she did most of the work herself. The menu, which was never complicated, was written on a blackboard on the wall. Wandering musicians often played there for the few pennies they could collect from the customers, and Rosalie usually gave them a glass of wine. I remember being taken there in 1923 by a friend, when the festivities in that hot, crowded room lasted until well after eleven at night.

Carmen, who still lives with her cat in the rue de la Grande Chaumière, is another of the old models. She posed for Rodin for sixteen years, so she says. Anyway, she once had a fine collection of his sketches, most of which she gave to an American to sell for her in New York. She never heard from the American again.

Carmen is half Italian and half Spanish, and painters say she used to be a fine model, with an especially well-formed back.

"Posing is my profession," she will tell you. "I am not like these others girls who only pose in order to find a new lover." And she would take some difficult pose and hold it, without moving, for two hours at a time. However, if she thought you were not *sérieux* she would talk and talk, and there was no way to stop her.

Douanier Rousseau has left a strong impression in Montparnasse. The *douanier,* as his name implies, was a customs agent before he became a painter, but he always retained the title. Hiler once told me the story of how he started to paint, which I thought very interesting.

Félicien Rops and another painter and two models had been celebrating in the cafés of the Boulevard St. Michel, keeping it up, with much drinking, until five o'clock in the morning. At that hour they decided to go to the country to paint the models, nude, out-of-doors. So they fetched their paints and canvas and started along the quays toward the railway station.

Looking down, they saw Douanier Rousseau, who had been stationed for the night to guard a couple of barges with dutiable merchandise. Rops remarked to his friend that the *douanier* looked like a painter, and his friend agreed.

"Hey *douanier,*" said Rops, "can you paint pictures?"

"I don't know," said Rousseau, "I've never tried, much."

"Why don't you try, *douanier?*"

"I have no paints, just now."

So Rops and his friend thought it would be a good joke to see a *douanier* try his hand at painting. They descended to the lower quay, posed one of the models on the barge, and set Rousseau to work. They themselves, probably, went to sleep, a relaxation they undoubtedly needed. A few hours later Rousseau had completed his well-known "Gitane Endormie." Of course Rops and his friend still thought the whole business a joke.

"Fine, *douanier,* fine," they said. "You will be a great painter. You have a flair. You should work hard." And then, with many a laugh, they went off to the country.

But Rousseau took all this very seriously. He rented a studio near the rue Vercingétorix and worked hard, though most of the painters of his day thought his paintings ridiculous.

Once a group of painters who were in the habit of dining at the Café de Versailles, near the Gare Montparnasse, invited Rousseau as a joke. They called him the Man-who-paints-the-trees-before-the-sky, because it is obviously much easier to paint the sky first and then put in the trees against it. But Rousseau had his own ideas on that score. When Rousseau came to the dinner, they pinned a sign on his back, "To our dear master, from his pupils." This was in fun at the *douanier*'s two pupils, who were both old men. But the joke is now the other way, for none of the painters at that dinner is remembered today except the poor *douanier*.

Max Weber was an American painter whom Rousseau greatly admired; in fact he thought himself and Weber the geniuses of the day. When Weber returned to the United States the *douanier* went to the station with him. As the train was ready to leave, Rousseau felt called upon to make a great remark, a phrase that would live, but unfortunately he could think of nothing. Then, as the train pulled out, with a sudden inspiration he ran along the tracks and shouted up at Weber, "*N'oubliez pas la Nature,* Max!"—do not forget Nature!

Modigliani was a period nearer to Montparnasse as I knew it. He was very poor, but struggled on against enormous odds like the true bohemian that he was. He was very good-looking, with dark eyes and curly hair, and always wore a corduroy suit and knitted jersey. An unfortunate love affair embittered him with life, and in the end he showed too great a taste for drinking.

There is a tale that when Modigliani died, the cat that had been his most faithful friend jumped out of the window of his studio, killing itself at the very moment that the painter breathed his last at a hospital some distance away. Shortly afterward his young wife ended her life, too, by jumping from the sixth-floor window of her hotel.

Modigliani, like Zak, died a miserable death just as fame and success were within his grasp.

Soutine, the Russian painter, was very poor, like Modigliani, and often went without food for two or three days at a time. His close friend was Zborowsky, who usually fared better, for he was more commercially minded. Zborowsky often shared what he had with Soutine.

One summer Soutine buried himself in a small village in the

country near Paris, because living was cheaper there. Before leaving, however, he had given some drawings to a dealer on the rue La Boëtie. The dealer had thought nothing of the drawings, but, being a friend of Soutine's, had not known how to refuse them.

A few days later Doctor Barnes, the Philadelphia collector, happened in and was immediately struck with the fine quality of Soutine's work.

"These are excellent," he said. "They are magnificent. Where is the artist who made these drawings?" The dealer did not know. Only Zborowsky knew where Soutine was staying.

And so Zborowsky, when the news was brought to him, thought he would play a joke on his friend. He filled a large basket with the finest foods he could afford, vegetables, a steak, fruits, cheese, and wine, and took the train to the country. He found Soutine in misery, his money spent, and almost starving.

"See what I have brought you, Soutine," said Zborowsky. "We will have a fine feast! Build a fire in the stove! Let us eat!" And all the time Zborowsky was casting a greedy eye around the room to a corner where stood a number of the canvases and drawings. I will buy these drawings for a song, he thought, sell them to Barnes, and tell Soutine of it afterward.

"But I have no fire," said Soutine. "There is no wood, no coal, nothing."

"Very well," said Zborowsky, "I will go to the town and buy an alcohol stove. I will be right back."

But the town was some distance away and Soutine grew impatient. When Zborowsky returned he found Soutine huddled over a small fire which he was feeding with the wood and canvas of his paintings! In horror, Zborowsky told him the story and together they pulled from the fire what was left.

After Soutine was recognized and had money to spend, he invited Michonze to lunch in the Negresco in Nice, and when Michonze had ordered his meal, Soutine asked only for mint tea. "When I was poor, I had no food," he said, "and now that I am rich, I have no digestion."

Soutine always claimed that he had suffered much more than Modigliani. "I suffered terribly with fleas and bedbugs. They kept me awake all night. But Modigliani slept soundly without waking no matter how many attacked him!"

I have heard so many stories of poverty that one might imagine Montparnasse more as a poor farm than an art colony in the old days. Milvoj Uzlac is another who struggled hard for his convictions.

Uzlac was at Sarajevo when the Austrian archduke was shot in 1914, and he was accused, with others, of being in on the plot. Although he was never convicted, he spent the four years of the war in a Serbian prison. In order to pass the time, he and his cellmate improvised situations and conversation in order to forget for a moment their miserable state. For instance, they would imagine that they were two young dandies on their way to the opera. Now they were getting out of their carriage. Now they were showing their tickets. Now they were being ushered into a box. Now the curtain was rising.

"I have an improvement to suggest," said Uzlac's companion one day. "Let us pretend that you are a beautiful woman and that I am in love with you."

"I am not as strong as you," said Uzlac, "but I am more nervous. If you insist on expanding my game in that direction, I swear by my mother I will strangle you!"

When Uzlac came to Paris he lived with his wife in Malakoff, and they were very poor. On those rare times when he sold a picture, his wife always knew of it at once by his method of arrival. Looking out the window she would see three or four taxis drive up to the door. In the first would be Uzlac, in the second, his cane, in the third, his hat; and in the fourth, his coat!

Another story of Montparnasse, just before I went there, concerns a model named Jackie. She came from a conservative, bourgeois country family, who kept her carefully guarded for the day when she would marry the local village clerk. But Jackie had other ideas. In a spirit of high adventure she took some of her brother's clothes, dressed herself as a boy, and set out for Paris.

There she met three American painters who found her a good model and a pleasant companion. The three of them supported her in a modest way, sharing her as a model and letting her cook for them. She continued to wear her brother's clothes, for she did not want to be recognized by friends from home.

In the end, though, she came to like one of the painters better than the others, and she moved in with him in the easy manner of models and artists. He found considerable affection for her, too, and he showed it by buying her new clothes—women's clothes— a ring, and a bracelet.

But this was too much for Jackie. One day the painter returned to his studio to find a note scrawled across the title page of a French-English dictionary. It read: "I am going away. You are so good. I am so weak. You are too good. I cannot stand it! Jackie."

I knew another girl, too, who dressed in boy's clothes. In fact, she played the part so well that most of the Quarter thought she was a boy, and even after that there was some doubt about it, no one could be quite sure. She too had run away from a family in the country, had dressed in her brother's clothes, and come to Paris. She took the name of Fano Mesan, and we never knew her real name. Fano was sixteen when she left home with a burning passion to be a sculptor. In Paris she met a Canadian, with whom she lived for a year or more. Doubtless he knew she was no boy, but he said nothing. As a result many of his friends turned against him, thinking he had become "queer."

Fano worked very hard, and they say her sculpture showed great promise. Eventually she returned to her family, who relented and allowed her to study in a more conventional way. I saw her in the Dôme a year ago, a fine-looking woman—in her right clothes.

Another person who has grown into a legend since I have known the Quarter is Pascin, the American painter. He had a very curious mental attitude toward life, for he insisted on surrounding himself with the most stupid, boring people he could find. Some of his friends were positively immoral, even for artists! Pascin probably had such friends in order that he might feel superior to them. He lived in an absolutely negative atmosphere, yet he was able to paint fine pictures and do large numbers of drawings. He did these even when surrounded by his friends. His studio in Montmartre was usually crowded with hangers-on of "the great Pascin." There would be couples making love, others recovering from hangovers, some sleeping, some drinking, most of them making great noise, and in the middle, Pascin painting or drawing with absolute unconcern. It was these friends who stole most of his drawings.

Once Pascin and Kisling, another renowned painter, went to Marseilles to make sketches in the red-light district, a subject dear to many modern painters. But hardly had they set up their easels when inhabitants of the section knocked them over. It was impossible to work there. Finally a woman told them to see Toussaint, the big boss of the Old Port. Only with his permission could they work freely.

Toussaint is a short man, with wild Corsican eyes. He started in Algeria in a "nice respectable business in girls," as he phrases it. But the girls ran away and he was forced to take stronger steps to obtain a living. He came to Marseilles and became the undisputed king of the Old Port underworld. He had but two deep interests in life; the first, his beautiful daughter, whom he guarded severely from all intruders until the right man came along; the second, art. Toussaint had a keen appreciation of art. He looked with interest on the modern school as well as on the classical, and his art collection was largely devoted to the modern.

It was to this man that Pascin and Kisling applied. They were received with open arms. Toussaint presented them with the keys to his part of the city! Word was passed around, and from then on the two painters had but to whisper the name "Toussaint" for the inhabitants to fairly bow before them.

Toussaint, whose name means "All Saints," was said to have considerable political power in France at that time, even in the Chamber of Deputies.

In any case Toussaint and the painters became fast friends.

Other painters, introduced by Pascin and Kisling, went to Marseilles and received the same welcome. In return the painters gave Toussaint drawings and sketches which he treasured.

In 1925 or 1926 Pascin told me he was organizing a big party at a restaurant near the central markets of Paris. It was to be the introduction of Toussaint to Montparnasse. After the dinner the artists were to take their underworld king to the Dôme and other cafés, to give him the keys to Montparnasse as he had given them the keys to the Old Port in Marseilles.

About one hundred fifty artists went to the dinner. They dressed in their oldest clothes, artists' clothes, that they might in no way embarrass their guests by being too fancy. Prompt to the minute, Toussaint arrived with eight of his lieutenants, every one of them in full polish: frock coats, gray striped trousers, wing collars and spats, complete! The artists were amazed. So were the guests. Toussaint said he thought he had put himself in the hands of a gang of toughs! He was ready to run. But Pascin explained and the dinner was a great success. Of course everyone got drunk, and late the following afternoon some of the survivors straggled into my bar to tell me about it.

It was about three years after the Toussaint party that Pascin, alone for once in his studio, opened his wrists and hanged himself from the hinge of the door.

Student pranks are very much in the tradition of Montparnasse, though they are practiced far less often today than ten or twenty years ago. One story is of the Beaux Arts Academy on the day when prizes were to be awarded by the president of France. In the courtyard were drawn up, on either side, a mounted company of those gaily uniformed French troops, the *gardes républicaines*. As they were waiting for the president to arrive, several students leaned from one of the windows.

"Hey, there, *garde,* is it hot?" said one.

"Yes, a bit," replied the soldier.

"Have you ever seen a nude model, my friend?" continued the student.

"What's that? What's that?"

"Turn around, soldier, and see the beautiful nude model. Just lean on the windowsill. The model is really a beauty. She is posing for us and cannot hide if you look at her." The soldier was interested. He looked at his officer, who was paying no attention. He looked at the window, which was not far away. He could see in by standing in his stirrups.

"All right," he said, and turning, he rose up toward the window to see the beautiful nude girl. But as soon as his head went over the sill he felt himself seized by several strong arms and his face smeared with quantities of heavy blue chalk! He disengaged himself just in time to find the president of the Republic entering the courtyard and his comrades standing at attention!

Another story concerns the Académie Julian in the rue du Dragon. It was told me by Achilles Badi, the well-known Argentine painter. When a new pupil arrives he is called *le nouveau* (the new one) and is expected to do the little duties that occur from time to time in an art studio.

One dark day the *massier,* or head of the class, said to Badi, "You are the new one? All right. It is too dark here. Go next door to the electric shop and fetch a daylight reflector. Hurry."

Badi hurried. He found the shop and entered.

"I am from Julian's Academy and I want to borrow a daylight reflector, please!"

"What!" said the proprietor. "You devil! Get out of here and don't ever come back. Get out before I kill you!" And then, with a burning sensation behind, Badi felt himself rise into the air and land with a considerable thud in the middle of the rue du Dragon, amid the cheers of the other students of the Academy and all the neighboring tradespeople.

It seems that in the course of more than twenty years, almost every new student had been sent to that same shop to borrow a daylight reflector, a machine that could not possibly exist. During that period the shop had been in the hands of the same family, father and son, a family singularly lacking in sense of humor, for each student has made them more furious than the last!

In another academy there was formerly a *concierge* whose wit and sight were somewhat dulled with age. This good woman had a goldfish which she used to place on the sill of her window in good weather, that it might get the sun.

"It needs sun like a flower," she used to say.

One day some students lowered a hook and line from an upper window, caught the fish, fried it on a small stove, and then replaced it in the bowl. The poor woman was both amazed and hurt.

"But you shouldn't have left it in the sun," the students said. "When you leave a fish in the strong sunlight, naturally it gets cooked." To console her they bought another live fish, a white one which they dyed red. This time she did not put it in the sun, but hid it away in a dark corner. When next she took it out, however, she was amazed to find that it had turned white.

"That is your fault," said the students. "You kept it too wet. Everyone knows that dampness takes the color out of things!"

BAR RACKETS

Because people, when they drink too much, often lose the sharpness of their senses, the Paris bar was a favorite rendezvous for confidence men and tricksters of all kinds. In fact, all Paris was and, I believe, still is a happy hunting ground for them, despite the vigilance of the police. The barman always cooperated closely with the police, for they could be very valuable to him. Each bar paid a special tax to the city in return for which the police stood on call at a moment's notice to calm an unruly crowd. The sight of the dark blue uniform usually had a magic effect upon drunks and fighters.

The police, on the other hand, were not rough with the drunk, as they are in other countries, but usually took him out of the bar, walked him down the street, and then let him go, or put him in a taxi and sent him home. Of course if he fought them, they took him to the station, where he was likely to receive a bad beating.

One of the things that I soon learned in France was that one should never try to bribe a policeman, for a French policeman will not take money, and may even charge you with attempted bribery, a serious offense. The local men came to the bar from time to time and we always gave them a few drinks, but money—no! It is not that French policemen are so simon pure, but, since they travel in pairs, the one is always afraid of the other.

Barmen sometimes worked for the police, giving information and being paid for it or receiving favors in return. Or the bar might be visited from time to time by plainclothes detectives who came to spot any movement against the government, especially of a communistic nature.

About the confidence men and the card sharps the barman

could do little except warn the intended victim, and even that was dangerous. Of course if he knew that a certain person was a cheat or a thief, through personal knowledge, he could forbid the man to come to the bar, on the threat of making a complaint to the police, but he had to be very sure of his ground. And the tricksters did all they could to keep in with the barmen, always paying their bills promptly and giving large tips.

But my greatest difficulties were the women who stole or cheated in petty ways that annoyed everyone, yet, because they were women or because the amount was so small, no one would make a complaint. The gigolo business, too, was one closely connected with Paris bars. The gigolos were those handsome young men who lived off the dowager duchesses of America with well-filled pocketbooks and expensive jewels. In the old days the gigolo was looked down on, but later he became quite smart. An older woman was often proud to have her gigolo. Personally, I think this arrangement was quite fair. Why shouldn't an older woman pay to have a beautiful young man accompany her! I used to have many gigolos in my bar, and most of them were fine young men, well educated and well mannered, but penniless and without qualifications for serious work.

There were some, though, who took advantage of their ladies to steal money or jewels, but these usually operated in Montmartre. In such cases the woman rarely complained to the police, for fear the news would reach the ears of her husband at home. Instead, she usually took the next boat back to the protecting walls of the hometown and the arms of hubby!

But if the gigolos were a good lot, the girls who sold themselves to bar patrons were decidedly unscrupulous and even dangerous. They would stop at nothing to gain a few francs. That this money was passed on to some "lover" did not lessen their covetousness; it increased it. I never understood the mentality of these girls.

The story behind each one of them was much the same. She was the daughter of poor but honest peasants in the provinces. Life was a drudgery with little recreation, for the ambitious young men of the town had gone to work in the cities. Those that remained behind were generally stupid. She became restless. She decided to work in Paris. But after a few months as a clerk or seamstress, the bright lights led her to something else. At first, if she was attractive, she may have had a lover, and then another, and finally she found herself attached to some café or bar, making her living in the only way she could.

In my bar I did not want such girls. The type of client I had always catered to came to my bar to talk with his friends, to drink quietly, to meet people of his own class, and didn't want to be pestered with French *poules*. Of course, after a few drinks he might want such company, and then I suggested some other bar or a nightclub in Montmartre as a fitting place to continue the evening.

Unfortunately I could not prevent such women from coming in and I could not refuse to serve them, but I always tried to show them to a table, saying that women unaccompanied were not allowed to sit at the bar. If they saw an American or English woman alone at the bar I said she was waiting for her husband, which they did not believe, of course. Perhaps my clients would not have minded if I had had one or two around, but if I had had *any,* there would soon have been a crowd.

Then, too, if I had had *poules* they would have taken the clients away to other bars where they received a commission on the drinks or where there were rackets for extracting money from the suckers.

The relationship of the *poule* to the bar management varied in different establishments, but in general it was something like this: The barman was the banker for the girls. He allowed them to run up bills for drinks, cigarettes, and food on his responsibility. The cash register chits for these sums for each girl he kept under the bar. Along came a man, sat down at the bar, but none of the girls talked to him until the barman gave the signal. In the meantime the barman was sizing up the sucker. If he thought him a real sucker with much money, the barman turned him over to his own particular girl if she was around, or to another favorite of his. This was all accomplished by an elaborate system of signals and winks. The lucky girl then got to work, usually starting the conversation by asking the sucker for a light.

He then bought her a few drinks and they decided to leave. "I'm afraid I can't leave," she would say. "I am in debt to the barman." So, reluctant or eager, the poor boob had to ask the barman for her chits, which might have amounted to fifty francs or more. Part of this sum represented food or drinks actually consumed by the girl, while the rest were fake chits that the barman had added for his own profit. In addition, the barman got a fat tip, of course. In a bar that did a big business, with many girls, the barman's profits were considerable.

Naturally, many clients who knew the game objected to having these girls around and swore that they would never come back, though they usually did, at least once in a while. But the best clients for this type of bar were those who were out on one grand spree—gay Paree and all that—mostly tourists or French from the provinces.

Almost all the girls had, in turn, a man to whom they gave the money they earned and that was what I could not understand. They were always proud of their *maquereaux,* or pimps, each of whom often had three or four girls working for him at once. Each thought her man was madly in love with her, but he never was, and he would sometimes beat her if she failed to make sufficient money.

When the depression came, the number of *maquereaux* increased as it became a "smart" occupation in the underworld. Once I asked one of the *poules*: "Why do you look down on a man because he gives money to a girl, and call him a sucker, but look up to a man who takes it from girls?"

"Because," she said, "the *maquereaux* themselves are the biggest suckers in the world. They spend all their money on us in the easy-come, easy-go fashion." Well, it was a strange sort of reasoning!

Sometimes a girl and her *maquereau* worked together on a little special badger game of their own. The *maquereau* would hang around in the shadows outside the bar. When the girl left with a man, she would make a signal to him, and he would rush home, hiding under the bed or in a closet. When the sucker and the girl arrived, the *maquereau* would spring out and rush at him.

"What are you doing with my wife!" he would yell. The sucker was lucky if he left with even his clothes!

Then there was the "swell" *maquereau* who worked in the big Right Bank bars and hotels. He usually had but one girl, or at the most, two. He was often well educated, and the girl also. They had all the social graces. In this game there was no rough stuff, just the straight sale of "merchandise." After a man of this type had made his fortune he often moved to another city, married the girl, and settled down to conventional bourgeois life. I have known two or three who became, in later life, highly respectable!

Another game for fleecing the lambs was the two-girls-in-a-car racket. This did not exist in Montparnasse when I was there, but happened fairly frequently on the Right Bank. Two girls in a car drew up to the curb and asked a well-dressed man for a light. The good clothes of the girls and the fine appearance of the car gave him confidence. One of the girls suggested they have a drink together. He got in and they drove to "a little bar she knew of." Inside they had a drink or two under the kindly eye of a barman, a manager, and a waiter. When the bill was presented it totaled several hundred francs or even more. During the ensuing argument the girls slipped out. The man either paid or received a bad beating from the three employees, who were all husky men. If there were other "clients" in the place, they turned out to be part of the management too.

But don't let me discourage anyone from going to Paris. I am telling you only the worst. The French are as honest as any others, and doubtless rackets of this kind exist in all cities of the world. If there were more in Paris it was because so many foreigners went there with their pockets well lined and laid themselves open to just such vultures.

The English were always more easily taken in by petty rackets than were Americans, partly because they were less observing, partly because they had a greater reluctance to argue. The American was constantly expecting to be "gypped" and was not afraid to make a fuss if he thought he had been cheated. On the other hand, once a trickster had gained the confidence of an American, the latter would go a long way with him.

A confidence game of sorts that I saw in Montparnasse several times was the inheritance racket. This was always played by women, and it usually lasted for a long time. There were around the bars men who had steady and sometime sizable incomes in their own right, who, because of too much drink, dope, or as a result of an unhappy love affair, were letting themselves go on the sure path to the grave. I never had a bar without one or two of these. One day such a man would pick up with a clever girl who made no effort to stop his drinking, yet made herself very companionable. He didn't fall in love with her—she would not have wanted that—but she pretended to be in love with him, all the time pushing him farther and farther down. She was scheming, of course, to obtain a will from him in her favor.

Dope always played a certain part in the life of Montparnasse, though there were comparatively few of the crowd that took it regularly. I have never tried dope and I don't think I ever will, but I have heard it discussed many times over the bar. For hopheads usually frequent the bars if only to make others believe that they don't take dope. A real doper doesn't drink alcohol because he has no taste for it. I have come to know them by little mannerisms and particularly by their eyes, which are usually slightly popped, with big pupils and yellowish whites. Those who take cocaine are constantly sniffing, some almost snorting. They are always very nervous. I knew one girl who jumped slightly every time she sniffed, and as she sniffed most of the time, she was constantly bouncing up and down on her chair. Hopheads usually start with cocaine because it requires no paraphernalia such as is needed for opium. They never take it in the bar, but disappear for a moment and come back greatly stimulated, more talkative and more clear minded. It has a great effect on the imagination. Many of the hopheads I have known have been decided intellectuals, who took it to stimulate them in their work. This is especially true of writers and painters.

It is not until they are far gone that they begin to use a needle, and then I am afraid of them, especially the women. Some of them go temporarily insane and are no longer responsible. If crossed in any way they frequently become violent. There is another type on which dope has the contrary effect, making them heavy but happy. They will sit in a corner and grin for an hour at a time.

The attitude of the French police is well-known. They make little effort to stop the sale of drugs to those who are already addicted, but do everything to prevent the initiation of new converts. Sometimes the addicts are arrested and jailed in an effort to cure them of the habit, but mostly they are allowed to do as they please.

I remember a wealthy Chicago family who had an apartment in fashionable Passy. The children used to give big dope parties to which many Montparnassians were invited, regular orgies of ether and cocaine. The head of the police finally made a personal call upon the parents, advising them to take their children away from Paris, which they did. One of my clients told me of a party he went to at this same house. He arrived to find a score of these youngsters crowded into a small room which swam with a reek of ether like an operating room in a hospital. The invitation he had received was for "cocktails," and he knew nothing of the dope until he arrived. The parents were fully aware of the situation, but did nothing to prevent it, though they themselves did not take dope of any kind.

This same man told me of buying some dope for a woman friend, and how he went about it.

"First I went to a bar in Montmartre," he said, "where I had seen many hopheads and asked the manager if he could procure some dope for me.

" 'Dope!' he said, 'I know nothing of dope. Don't come to me for drugs!—However, if I hear anything, I'll let you know.'

"So he took my phone number, but it was more than a week before I heard from him.

" 'Come in and have a drink,' he said, 'you haven't been in for a long time.' So I had a drink or two at an appointed hour when the bar was well filled. I asked him again about the dope, but he was vague. Perhaps. He didn't know anyone who handled dope. Well, perhaps. Of course I knew that I had been called there to be examined by dope peddlers, who must have been among the clients in the bar. I had no suspicion of who they were, however.

"The next day a strange female voice called me by phone.

" 'I am a friend of Monsieur,' she said, mentioning the bar manager's name. 'Could you meet me today at three?' She named a bar in Montparnasse. When I met her she had the cocaine in her bag and handed it over as soon as I gave her the money. Once they felt sure of the purchaser, she said, the actual delivery was very easy."

A more ridiculous story is that of an American woman who was told she could buy dope at the Moulin Rouge in Montmartre. Jumping into a taxi, she drove up to the main entrance of the dance hall. It happened to be a rainy night, and upon her arrival the doorman, with his large red umbrella, came to the cab.

"I want some cocaine," she said. "Can you get it?" He was somewhat astonished, but nevertheless quick-witted.

"I do not sell it myself," he replied, "but I think I can get it nearby for you. However, I will need a deposit before they will let me take it away." She gave him five hundred francs and he disappeared around the corner. A few minutes later he reappeared with a small package neatly wrapped and tied.

"The price," he said, "is eight hundred francs, so you still owe me three hundred." Happy, she gave him the three hundred francs and two hundred more as a tip, and drove home. The package contained an antiseptic powder. Had it been cocaine it would have been enough for a whole army!

The police effort against the dope traffic is largely directed against the peddlers, though they are hard to catch. Another barman told me about being in an American bar in the rue Edouard VII when the police surrounded the place to catch a peddler who was dining there. But he was warned and hurriedly disposed of all the dope he had on him in the lavatory. When the police broke in, he was arrested, but released the same day for lack of evidence. For a first offense a dope peddler gets six months, which seems very little.

Most of the dope in Montparnasse is sold by girls, some of whom act as stool pigeons for the police in order to have protection. Dope is something I have never handled in any form and I will always keep away from it, for it has been the ruin of many persons I have known.

MORE PERSONALITIES

Montparnasse was a mutual admiration society and the members delighted in each other's colorful characteristics. When a new personality came to the Quarter he was the rage for a short time, everyone quoted him, everyone laughed over his stories.

One such newcomer was Guy Arnoux, the French illustrator and painter, who did some of the murals on the Ile-de-France. His studio was a veritable museum of costumes, knickknacks, lead soldiers, models of ships, old bottles, telescopes, globes, saddles, and hundreds of other things, a truly remarkable collection. Guy would often wear the costumes, as he liked to dress up, sometimes as a cowboy, or as an officer in the navy, or as a cook, with pots and pans tied from his waist. He attended most of the costume balls of the Quarter, and was always a big success.

Guy is the only man who has ever drunk Dôme beer at the Sélect, and it happened this way. Monsieur Sélect, as he was called, noticed that Guy was fond of setting groups against each other and thus causing fights in which Guy himself did not take part. And so Monsieur Sélect told Guy that he would not be served in the future. Nevertheless, Guy continued to sit on the *terrasse* and Monsieur Sélect retired to his lair near the cash register. Hardly had he left when Guy offered a waiter a substantial tip to bring him a beer from the Dôme. When Monsieur Sélect discovered the ruse he was furious, but powerless to prevent it!

One night Guy was in my bar when his friend Paul Poiret, the celebrated dress designer, came in. At another table were a group of English and Americans, and among them Jacko, a Frenchman

142

who spoke English with a perfect Oxford accent. Whether it was true or not, Guy thought the Anglo-Saxons were making fun of Paul Poiret's big figure and somewhat eccentric dress. The upshot was that Guy informed Jacko in English that he'd do well to return to his own country, to leave France to the French, for what could a mere foreigner know of the respect due to a great artistic figure of Paris like Paul Poiret! The fight was on.

In the end Guy rushed for the telephone, called the police, and then rushed up to his studio. When he returned he held in his hand two large pistols and I thought there was going to be real trouble. However, the police arrived at the same time, disarmed him, and found that the pistols were not loaded anyway. At the police station it came out that Jacko was really French, a fact which amazed Guy so much that he completely forgot his resentment. They returned together to the bar and became the best of friends!

A great place for friends to gather in the days when I first went to Montparnasse was the *bougnat* (shop selling wine, coal, and wood, usually with a zinc bar but no tables) on the corner of the rue Campagne-Première, owned and run by an old Auvergnat, Père Londiche. One day a retired jockey named Miller happened in, liked the place, and forthwith arranged to take it over. To the owner he was to pay sums at regular intervals.

Jockey Miller made the place a success at once. It was he who introduced to the Quarter the singer Les Copeland, whom I described in an earlier chapter. Miller made money, plenty of money, and promptly lost it in gambling, of which he was very fond. Finally he left the café, poorer than when he went there, and Père Londiche took over the management again.

But Père Londiche saw that there was far more money to be made with this new crowd than with the old *bougnat,* so he looked around for a likely manager who would make much money for him. He found Hilaire Hiler, painter, writer, authority on costume, pianist, singer and, suddenly, café manager. Hiler redecorated the Jockey, as it was now called, and the paintings on the outside

FOUJITA

from a drawing by Hilaire Hiler

today, though somewhat faded, are the same that Hiler painted in 1923.

Under Hiler's sway, with Les Copeland's talent, the Jockey was a huge success. It was very informal and usually very gay and crowded.

An important member of the Jockey was Bangs, the colored drummer, who married a white French girl. When their baby arrived it was absolutely white, much to his delight. On the least provocation he would pull out a picture of Baby Bangs. "See dat chil'? She sure am white!"

An old-timer of the Les Copeland type was John Mahon, who spent most of his life in the oil fields of Oklahoma and Mexico. The stories he told of oil days in the Southwest would fill a book, stories of extraordinary luck, both good and bad, of tough *hombres* and wicked *señoritas*.

I remember particularly his tale of a whisky in Arizona years ago named Four Roses—a good drink, he said, and much stronger than the "watery" liquor they served in Paris. Once, John said, he went into a new town, stood at the bar, and asked for three fingers of Four Roses.

"Sorry, John," said the bartender, who knew him, "we ain't got no Four Roses. In this town we drink Five Roses. It's better. More kick, kinda!"

"Sure," said John, "give me the Five Roses. Set up the bar, too." In the room were a dozen or more men only too glad to have a free drink.

Later it was suggested that John, who was flush that day, set them up to another round.

"No," said John, "but I'll buy you a whole bottle and you can drink it among you. Hey, bartender, give me a bottle of Five Roses."

"Sure," said the bartender.

"I'm going to give it to the boys," added John.

"What?" said the bartender, "you're going to give a whole bottle to those few boys? No sir! I'm sorry, John, I can't sell you no bottle of whisky today."

"Why not? What's the matter?"

"Sorry, John. I can't have those men drinking a bottle of Five Roses in my place."

Finally John got the bottle on the condition that the boys take it across the square to the courthouse steps. There they consumed it and later John bought another bottle. Never had he seen whisky with such lightning in it! During the following twenty-four hours all business was stopped in the town except the bar. The whole town was in an uproar, shooting revolvers, yelling, screaming and bellowing, playing practical jokes and generally raising the devil! It was as though the whole town had gone insane. And for the twenty-four hours that followed this, the town was like dead, for everyone slept soundly.

Handsome Homer Bevans, called "The Emperor," was one of the most loved characters of Montparnasse. Deep-voiced Homer sat around the cafés, not talking very much, his big hands spread on the table before him. His nickname was given him by a Spanish journalist, who left this message for him one day: "If you see the Emperor, will you tell him that all his domestic servants are awaiting him at the Sélect!"

Homer had come to France to study sculpture but he had not done very much with it. At first he worked, I believe, and did, among other things, the bust of a beautiful girl. Several times he was asked to name the model, so that others might sculpt or paint her, but he always replied that he did not know. Or he would say, "I made her up out of my head."

One night in the Dingo, Homer, who was nothing if not passive, suddenly came to animated life. "Look!" he almost shouted, "Look! My model! See? My girl!" He pointed to an American girl sitting at the bar. She was surprised and somewhat embarrassed by this sudden attention, especially as she had just arrived from America and knew almost no one present. Homer rushed over to her. "You are the girl!" It seems that Homer had really imagined the face of the girl in the statue and had for years been looking for an original to ascribe it to. A novel way to do portraits!

Homer once met Harold Stearns in the street, and stopped him, saying, "I don't mind you, but I wish you would look after your horse. I was going into the Vikings one night and he bit me. I knew he wanted a drink, so I took him in and bought him one!"

Harry Kemp, poet and playboy, was one of the familiar figures of the Jockey. It was he who organized the famous wine parade, with the assistance of Hiler and Vernon Caughell, Hiler's partner at the Jockey. (Caughell later married the girl who was known far and wide as "the Goldfish," because of her red hair, which she wore in bangs!)

The wine parade was to be a march of the bohemians of Montparnasse to join the bohemians of Montmartre in a giant protest against prohibition in the United States. As a stimulus to enthusiasm, a French winegrowers' association had provided many barrels of good red and white wine free of charge.

And so the parade started. I got up early that day just to see it, for it left Montparnasse about eleven in the morning with two hundred or more artists tramping behind the romantic figure of Harry Kemp. If they had had the parade in the afternoon the whole Left Bank would have been there, I suppose.

At the head of the procession was a huge banner saying, "It shall be dry no more! It shall rain always!" Among the marchers was Colbert, the American Indian, who was in full regalia, feathers and all.

As a march through the city, the parade was not a great success, however, due to a pernicious idea of one of the bar hounds. He and a friend hailed a taxi shortly after the procession started.

"We will go ahead for a drink," he said, "and then when you march by we will join the ranks again." It was a fine idea for a few, but almost at once everyone conceived the same idea, leaving no parade to "march by"!

And so only a few ever actually climbed the Montmartre hill, although most of them got there in taxis, already feeling pleasantly stimulated. In the Place du Tertre were the bohemians of Montmartre, and (Hurrah!) the barrels of wine. Lucien Boyer, the "mayor" of the Free Commune of Montmartre, was the master of ceremonies, though in a short time there was little left of them.

Kemp made a fine speech in English, which practically no one understood, but which was loudly applauded.

"I don't care for my life!" he said, "I am a poet! I will jump out of an airplane with a parachute and a bottle of French wine over the Channel. I don't care for my life! If I am rescued by a passing boat, all right. If not, it does not matter! I am a poet. It will be big publicity for French wine and the cause against prohibition."

This project was never carried out, however, because Kemp had a cold and couldn't go!

Someone who is still seen in Montparnasse, I believe, is Louis Tyhanyi, the deaf-mute Hungarian painter. When I went to the Dingo he was there frequently with his friend Count Karolyi.

"James, mix a strong one for Louis," Karolyi would say, "he needs a strong one." It was a little game they played, to make Tyhanyi tight.

A few years ago Tyhanyi went to the United States, where he had a very difficult time getting around. First he was landed on Ellis Island and was held because he could not explain himself. Then, once in New York, he was constantly being arrested for the same reason. He knew not a word of English, of course. So Nagouchi, a Japanese-American friend of his, painted a sign which he carried around with him, reading: "I am deaf and dumb," and then when people saw that they would try to give him pennies! But at least they understood why he didn't talk.

And who could forget Doc Mahoney, the wittiest man in Montparnasse? Doc was considered an excellent physician and he treated many of the poorer artists of the Quarter free of charge. I believe he once was highly rated for his research in cancer.

But Doc had lived many years in Montparnasse, following the death of his wife, and finally took up wit as a profession. He always referred to himself as little Miss Minnie Mahoney, the Irish girl of culture whom God forgot.

Once I was sitting in front of the Dôme with him when two small French sailors went by.

"Look, Jimmie," said Doc, "just what the doctor ordered—seafood!"

Doc once lived with an American couple named Woods, and when Mr. Woods went to America on a trip, Doc was seen in the cafés with Mrs. Woods. On introducing himself he always said, "We are the widows Woods!"

Foujita, the Japanese painter who has been so successful, could be found at the Parnasse at least once or twice a week, a strange little man with his bobbed and banged hair, his gold-rimmed glasses, his earrings, and eccentric clothes. At that time he had just divorced Fernande Barry and was married to Yuki, another French girl. Fernande had married Koyanagui, another Jap and a friend of Foujita's. The four of them were often seen together.

Foujita gave large parties at the Parnasse, especially before the Quat'Z'Arts ball, when he would come in a brief costume which exposed his greatly tattooed body, for he had been a sailor before becoming a painter.

A group that I often had in the Parnasse was Sutton Vane, the author of *Outward Bound,* his sister, Sybil, and Norman Jacobsen, that almost ghostly figure for whom everyone felt so sorry because he was so thin, though actually he was quite healthy, I believe.

Norman had a dog named Dingo, a regular bar hound who knew every one of his master's haunts in Montparnasse. Many a time I have seen Dingo go from bar to bar, enter each, make a tour of inspection, and then trot on to the next until he found his master.

This was about the time that Sutton Vane's dramatic success was being produced in French at the Studio des Champs Élysées, and Norman became very much interested in plays too. He and Sybil made some puppets and before a very enthusiastic audience produced a puppet play called *Green Sleeves,* which they themselves had written.

Norman and I would have long talks at the bar about the stage in England as I knew it through my father, who was an actor, and particularly about my favorite comedian, Harry Weldon, who wrote and acted his own sketches. Norman was writing a sketch for Hiler and myself, a bar scene in which we were to be knockabouts, with lots of sliding down ladders. We rehearsed several times, but nothing came of it in the end because, I think, Norman went away. We were to have traveled with it in England, and I was very sorry it did not go through.

Allen Ullman, whom you could recognize by his mop of red hair, claimed to be the most Montparnassian American in the world, for he was born in the building over the Dôme when that institution was still a little bistro. He bore a striking resemblance to Harpo Marx of the Marx Brothers. Once, in Nice, Harpo walked right up to Allen on the street. "Oh look," Harpo said, pointing his finger, "there I am! How do I do? How am I? I haven't seen myself for a long time!"

Harpo, incidentally, is very fond of practical jokes or jokes of a dramatic nature. On one occasion in Nice he dressed himself as a woman and lay on a chaise longue beside a swimming pool, lazily fanning himself. He lay thus for some twenty minutes and then suddenly jumped into the pool, screaming, "I will end it all! O my God!"

One of the subjects of controversy in Montparnasse for many years was Harold Stearns, the man who preferred to be a racehorse expert rather than (perhaps) a great writer. Harold came to Montparnasse to escape, so he said, the fine reputation he had gained in America with the publication of his first two books. He was disgusted by the praise and coddling he had received. In Paris he led an erratic life, working just enough to keep himself going, and developing his great interest in horses.

Finally he was offered the job of "Peter Pickem" on the *Chicago Tribune,* to report horse-racing events and predict the winners. He was very successful at this, picking four or five winners out of six, and himself often betting on outsiders whose names were not indicated in the paper. Later he went to the *Daily Mail* to do the same job, but shortly afterward he became very ill and was forced to resign. He, like so many other Americans mentioned in this book, now lives in New York.

Harold afterward wrote a book of memoirs which was published by Lee Furman under the title of *The Street I Know.*

Another good friend of mine was Douglas Golding, who wrote

much of his book *La Façade* in Pirelli's. In that book I was the barman, though he made me out to be rather pro-English, and consequently anti-American. But really I am an internationalist. I like persons for themselves and not for their nationalities. I would like an Australian bushman just as well as an Englishman, if he was a good fellow.

Until I came to Paris, I had seen very few Negroes, and I had not yet heard of the white man's superiority. Once in the Dingo a colored man came to see old Bruce, the cook. When he came in, most of the clients got up and went out, much to my astonishment. I asked Wilson if there was a fire or something, and he explained how some English and Americans are too self-conscious to sit in the same room with a Negro.

There was one exception to this rule, however, and that made it seem stranger. Claude McKay, colored musician and writer, was welcomed by a large number because of his very fine personality and charm. He and I became excellent friends. Claude's autobiography *A Long Way from Home* has recently been published.

The only living painter whose pictures hung in the Louvre during his lifetime was Claude Monet, the aged artist who resided in his famous house and garden in Giverny. Monet's daughter married an American painter named Butler, and their son, Jimmy Butler, was a popular figure in Montparnasse for a long time.

Jimmy is a thorough woodsman, a man who keeps as close to nature as he can, camping and hunting through the summer, even making some of his own clothes. "I think I have Indian blood in me," he told me once, "I feel the same instincts." To see him squatting on his heels like an Indian in the atmosphere of the Dingo was funny indeed!

There were so many well-known writers and artists in Montparnasse that a list of them would be a veritable *Who's Who* of talent. Most of them were good friends of mine, but here I can only mention those about whom I remember particular and printable incidents. Mary Butts, the English writer, was one whom I used to see frequently, usually accompanied by Mary Reynolds, the girl with the Mona Lisa smile and hair prematurely white. Once Mary

Butts told me about a portrait of a Colonel Butts painted by Holbein, which had been in her family for a long time. She said the family had been offered eighty thousand pounds for it!

"You know, James," she said, "I'll tell you a secret! There are about five brush strokes in the left-hand corner that were done by a pupil of Holbein's. You mustn't tell anyone! That's a big secret."

Gwen Le Gallienne, daughter of the writer and half sister of the actress and herself a painter, lived in the Quarter for many years. One year she held an exhibition at the American Library, and on the opening day two portraits were stolen under very mysterious circumstances. One was a portrait of Gilbert White, the painter. The papers were full of the mystery of the robbery and it gave Gilbert a grand opportunity of making wisecracks to the reporters about the person who wanted a portrait of him so badly that he had to steal it!

Later the pictures were found in the cloakroom of a railway station and there were some so unkind as to suggest that the robbery was staged for publicity purposes, though this was indignantly denied by Gwen herself.

It is said that the Duke of Windsor, then prince of Wales, visited Montparnasse in 1924. I may have served him, for all I know, because he was traveling incognito and there was a strict taboo on making any greater fuss for him than for anyone else. I do remember, however, recognizing him in Jed Kiley's place in Montmartre one night. He was accompanied by three or four friends and the evening was progressing nicely when the waiters and cooks took the opportunity to demand an increase in wages. They knew that the prince was present, of course. Jed took a firm hand, said he would not be bullied simply because there was a distinguished guest present, so the help walked out!

Jed rose to the occasion magnificently. He stopped the music, told everyone the circumstances, and called for volunteers so the night's gaiety could go on. The response was immediate, and even the prince was anxious to help, though his friends would not let him. The doors were locked, some of the men acted as waiters, an American girl made sandwiches in the kitchen, and everyone had a glorious time until three o'clock in the morning!

What a mixture Montparnasse was! In the same bar at the same time I might see such an assortment as Brancusi, the bearded exponent of modern sculpture; Vassilieff, the Russian creator of the doll craze, who still has her fantastic studio-restaurant in the rue Froidevaux; Jack Dean, Fanny Ward's husband, who was noted for his fine generosity; F. Scott Fitzgerald and his wife, Zelda, who pretended to look down on Montparnasse but came there frequently nevertheless; Bill Bullitt, who has since returned to France as American ambassador, and his former wife, Louise Bryant, who became so interested in aviation that she insisted on wearing the uniform of a French aviation officer in the Dôme; Rupert Fordham, the English painter, dressed in the red sailcloth costume of a Breton fisherman and carrying in his pocket bird bread and a bottle of olive oil; Stephanus Eloff, sculptor grandson of General Kruger of Boer War fame; Helen Havemeyer, granddaughter of a famous New York mayor; Pierre Loving, standby of all art colonies; Ludwig Lewisohn with his coterie of noisy admirers; Erskine Gwynne, one of the Vanderbilts and a leading socialite of both banks; Aisha, the mulatto model whose portrait hangs among the immortals in the Luxembourg; Nathan Asch and his celebrated father, Scholom; and perhaps even Jack Dempsey, though I remember only his coming once or twice, when, seemingly awestruck, he hardly opened his mouth. Some of them knew each other; some didn't, but it was no matter, for they were all friends after the third drink!

Djuna Barnes, the writer, was one of my good friends who brought me many clients. She is very much of a lady and well liked. She was the cause of what Hemingway calls my "greatest socking exploit" in Montparnasse.

It happened one night at the Sélect. Miss Barnes, Thelma Wood, and another girl were having some drinks on one side of the room, and near them were Bob McAlmon and Ian Meyers. It was my night off and I came in for a quick one before bed. I think the six of us must have been the sole occupants of the bar, but there may have been others.

And then came swinging into the bar an internationally known American newspaperman. It might hurt him in business were I to give his name, so I will call him Frank. He was roaring drunk. Focusing on Djuna, he lunged toward her and without ceremony not only sat beside her, but began pawing and mauling her in a fashion no gentleman should use.

Thelma Wood came over to me.

"Jimmie," she said, "please do something about Frank. Hit him or move him or something, right now."

I hesitated. Frank was one of my best clients. In the end I got him to another table, bought him a drink, and tried to turn his attention away from Miss Barnes. But it wouldn't be turned.

"Let's go out on the terrace," I said, "and pretend to fight. Just an imitation fight. We won't really hit each other." By doing that I thought the girls would feel better and I could get Frank away. But it didn't work that way. Djuna Barnes followed us out and let forth at Frank a piece of her mind. Then, in the twinkling of an eye, for Frank was fast, he knocked down Miss Barnes with a well-placed blow to the chin. In a few seconds the other two girls, Bob McAlmon, and Ian Meyers were all sprawled on the sidewalk. But Bob jumped up at once, knocked Frank down, and sat on him.

"Let me up!" said Frank. "Let me up! I'll behave." After solemn promises Bob let him up. But he had hardly got to his feet when he again let forth with both fists at the girls, Bob, and Ian. This must stop, I thought. So, wading into the fight, I brought up all the force I had. Three times I knocked Frank down, leaving a gash, that required three stitches later, in his face. The third time he could hardly stand. But he could talk. He swore that he would have me deported from France, that he would hound me all my life.

Then I took him to the lavatory and washed the blood from his face and later Carmen, and Olga, two of the French girls who hung around the bar, took him to a pharmacy for proper care. The next day he did not remember who had hit him, but when he found out I do not think he held it against me.

ALCOHOLICS CAN'T HELP IT

The man or woman who drinks to excess is always severely blamed by the more righteous. Why doesn't he stop? says the holy one. *I* don't need liquor to keep me going; why does he? Where is his willpower? But my experience of dipsomaniacs—and I have, of course, known a great many of them—is that their problem is not so simple. I have been, I think, quite successful in handling drunks because I have been drunk so many times myself. I have sympathy for them, and they respond to that treatment like no other. Criticism always makes them worse. In my own case I have found, after much experience, that I cannot drink at all without having it affect me seriously; and so I have forced myself to stop drinking entirely, except for occasional sprees. But the vast majority of my clients in Paris were quite capable of drinking in moderation without going to extremes or without damage to their health or morals.

There are two classes of persons who get drunk frequently. The first group is small, being those who, like myself, cannot stand even a little alcohol without being affected. In serving such persons I usually make their drinks a little lighter so that they can keep up with their friends without getting ahead of them.

The second group are the real dipsomaniacs, those who cannot resist drinking because of a craving. Behind this craving will always be found, I think, some deep-rooted mental or physical cause. Sometimes this state is produced or aggravated by a severe mental depression, an unhappy love affair often, or the loss of money. It may be a temporary condition that passes after a few months or less, or it may be permanent. Drinking is a relief from the responsibilities of life, an outlet from reality, an escape that may be vitally necessary in order to avoid suicide.

In other cases the dip has some organic trouble that may or may not be known. Let me tell you the stories of a few.

Jack was the son of wealthy parents, with the background of all they could offer him. But liquor he simply could not resist. His parents did everything possible to cure him, even to having him live for a while with Doctor Adler, the psychoanalyst. It did him no good. In desperation they had him undergo the Keeley cure, which was effective in that he could no longer swallow alcohol, or if he did it would not stay down. He seemed on his way to recovery, so he was sent to France for a change and a rest.

The first time Jack came to my bar, I was surprised to have him order a glass of milk with rum in it. That was a new drink to me. I served him. He took very little rum. During the next few months, however, he gradually increased the amount until he was able to intoxicate himself again. By the same slow, painstaking process, he reeducated his taste to brandy, gin, and whisky. Soon he was back to where he had started!

It was not lack of willpower that ruined Jack. In fact, he showed his willpower and perseverance when he nullified the effects of the Keeley cure! It was a tumor on the brain, which the doctors finally discovered. He was only seeking escape from something of which he had no conscious knowledge, but which must have hurt his subconscious being very severely. When he found that doctors could not help him, poor Jack committed suicide.

Another such case was Sally. She too came from wealthy parents. In Montparnasse she made herself very unpopular because of her mania for insulting everyone in sight for no reason whatsoever. She came to Paris to paint, but I don't know when she had any time for that, for she was drinking constantly, a real dip. Later she told me that she had been kicked in the head by a horse when a small child, and I have always thought that must be, somehow, the cause of her drinking.

Josephine was another alcoholic of this type. She blamed her father, who, she claimed, had violated her when she was a small child, though she really did not know whether this was true or not. She not only drank, but she suggested herself into tuberculosis which would come on her in spells, always when life was becoming complicated or when she felt the need for sympathy. There was no doubt of her having the illness and actually suffering! It was real enough while it lasted.

Friends told me that she rather overdid this "escape" method in New York, where she became a frequent patient in Bellevue Hospital. The nurses and interns in the alcoholic ward of that famous institution eventually became tired of her constant visits, so one night they changed from the kind and sympathetic treatment they had given her before, and became very severe, making her undergo a routine that was far from pleasant.

Thereafter, when she became difficult to handle, all one had to do was to pretend to put through a phone call to Bellevue and, like magic, she was cured of what ailed her.

One of the mad drinkers of Montparnasse was a young Irishman named Mike, a gentle, retiring soul when sober, and a savage, ripsnorting fiend when drunk. He was very much in love with a girl from the Middle West, and most of the time he was completely absorbed in her. But once he had a few Pernods under his belt, the girl was as much ignored as though he had never seen her. She, at first, used to demonstrate with him, try to get him to stop drinking and go home. But she soon gave that up. It only made him worse. So whenever she saw he was really drunk, she would quietly get up and go home. Next day he would be around to her hotel as soon as he got up, full of apologies.

One night he had been especially difficult, first at my bar and then at the Dôme, upsetting tables and punching total strangers. His girl could do nothing with him and he was last seen rushing down the Boulevard du Montparnasse as though ten devils were after him instead of inside him.

He has no memory of what happened then, but around four in the morning he came to from a gentle sleep to find himself under a rosebush! It was raining lightly and he felt chilly. Rising, he saw that he was in a garden, a very beautiful garden, and before him was a house. Slowly, his mind fixed only on the fact that he was cold, he walked toward the house. The front door was unlocked and he walked in, but had difficulty in finding the light.

In a moment or two it was turned on for him, however, and a man in a bathrobe stood before him.

"I'm cold," said Mike, in English.

"Come in here," said the man in the same language. Mike went into the sitting room, letting the man take off his wet coat.

"I'm hungry," said Mike.

"Well, lie down on the couch and I'll get you some food," said the man. Mike obeyed. And now appeared a woman who came forward, arranged Mike's pillow, and generally made him comfortable. She then went to the kitchen and reappeared a little later with a tray of eggs, hot buttered toast, and coffee. Mike ate the food, already feeling much better, though his head ached badly. For the headache they gave him two aspirins.

"I'm sleepy," he said. Fixing a comfortable bed on the couch, the couple opened the window, turned out the light, and left him to a sound slumber.

The next day he woke toward afternoon, alone in the room, and feeling much better.

"Where am I?" He said aloud, and at once the couple of the night before entered from an adjoining room. "Who are you? Where am I?" He struggled to say it in French.

And then the story was told. The couple were Americans who had seen Mike enter the garden, had realized that he was drunk, had seen him deliberately lie down under the rosebush. Later they had been waked by his opening the door, and had, quite simply, offered their care and hospitality to a fellow countryman. Mike had no memory of entering the house, of the food, or anything until he woke the next afternoon. Nor did he ever learn how he got to this house, which was in a suburb of Paris some miles from Montparnasse!

Peggy was another interesting case, for the effect of her dipsomania was to cause her to live entirely in the past. She was one of the most beautiful girls I have ever known and I felt very, very sorry for her, and still do. She came from a British dominion, where her father was a barrister and her grandfather had been prime minister. The lure of the stage took her to London, where she sang and danced successfully in several theaters, and where she met a British officer with an imposing title. They were married and lived happily together for several years. She seemed very fond of the son who was born to them.

With maturity she grew more beautiful and more popular, living in a continual round of parties and attention until half of London was at her feet. Her head was turned by such a wealth of personal success, so that she began to think herself capable of anything. When she fell in love with a Canadian, her husband made no effort to interfere, though he was still in love with her. With a gallant gesture, he gave a large party at which she was formally turned over to the Canadian!

The latter returned to Canada for a month or so in order to settle some business matters before making arrangements for their marriage, but on the way back he died of a fever. Peggy was deeply hurt and turned for consolation to drink. She still lives in the days when she and the Canadian first knew each other, and, drunk or sober, nothing can bring her to a realization of the present. If her mind could once be brought into today, she would be cured, I think. Many have tried very patiently and seriously, but it seems quite impossible.

I first saw Peggy in the Abbaye de Thélème in Montmartre in 1921, when I was assistant waiter there, and was greatly impressed with her beauty. I also saw her later at the Hole-in-the-Wall with a British journalist who made a great effort to help her, without success.

It was six years later that she came to Montparnasse and I came to know her well. I could not take my eyes off this woman who was not only beautiful but always stunningly dressed. Many of my clients, who had no special desire to know her, would be content to look at her for hours at a time.

Of course Peggy always had a train of men behind her. On some she bestowed her favors with great freedom, especially on those who would take her on gay parties, for she loved good times and drinking. Money held no interest for her, and if she ever caused a man to spend money too freely it was to help someone who had none. Many men tried to reform her, or at least bring her to a point of greater responsibility toward herself, but it was not possible, and they always left her in the end.

One of Peggy's worst habits was riding all over town in a taxi without a sou in her pocket to pay the fare, sometimes running up a bill of a hundred francs or even two. Often I would pay these bills, but that only encouraged her in it. In many cases she was taken to the police station, where she would pass the night until some admirer would appear with the necessary money. All the taxi drivers in Montparnasse knew her and some were very good about letting her have a day or two in which to find the money.

She had pet names for all her friends. Some of these names were amusing; such as Woofus Wambles for Wambly Bald, the *Chicago Tribune* columnist. Me she always called Angel Face or Babe Heart. One day she came into the bar and said, "James, Babe Heart, I noticed at the Ritz that they are serving extraordinary cocktails called Bacardis. Can you make them?"

Suddenly the door opened and a lusty-voiced taxi driver was demanding his money.

"Pay?" she said, "Pay? You frogs! We paid you in 1914. You have been paid many times. We paid with our lads and our money! Let there be another war and see if my boy will go or any of our people!" On these occasions I would pay the taxi and then she would turn to me.

"James, Angel Face, who are those people over there? They sound like my own people—real people!"

At other times, suddenly waking from memories of the past, she would say, "James, Angel Heart, who are these people, and where are we?" I think she honestly did not know.

One day she was taken to a police station on the Right Bank, where she was not known. When her bag was examined for her papers, it was found to contain a notice from the French government ordering her to leave the country a week earlier.

A few days later she left for Belgium, and after a considerable stay there was finally deported to England, where she has recently written her life story for a weekly paper. I am told, however, that she still lives in that glorious past from which she finds no escape.

Another group that formed an important part of Montparnasse life were the homosexuals. When I first went to Paris I had never heard of such people, and thought they must be a recent invention! Everyone told me differently, of course, but I don't think they had any in Manchester, where I was brought up.

As homos go, I prefer the women to the men—it seems more natural. In a bar the women are more quiet and reserved than the men, even though they wear mannish clothes. They are good, consistent drinkers but I have never seen one intoxicated, and they never make scandals in the bar. I have a great deal of respect for them.

The men are more boisterous and always more conspicuous because of their high, often shrill, feminine voices. They drink more than the women and are always more rowdy. Put two such men together and at once they must stage a show for their own fun and the benefit of the other present.

"My name is Kate," one will say, "and I'm just a little Soho sinner!"

"Now stop it, Kate," the other one replies, "if you don't stop, I'll let my back hair down." During all this there are many gestures of combing the hair, powdering the nose, even adjusting imaginary garters. I remember one pair on the Riviera who dressed alike, with white pullovers, blue trousers, blue sapphire rings, and rode around together in a light blue car.

I have always had a few among the clients of the bar. They are good spenders, generous, and usually very cultured, though always clowning. One very good client at the Falstaff was a wealthy American whom we will call Mr. Sharp. It was his pleasure to call everyone "monsieur," irrespective of nationality, and to indulge in a passion for flowers. One afternoon he brought a hundred or more roses to the bar. The Countess Eileen was the only woman there at that moment, so first he gave her a handsome bouquet. Then, one by one, he presented bouquets to all the men present. When he came to Homer Bevans, who was taking a little nap, he gave him an exceptionally large bunch and slipped a hundred-franc note into it, too.

Mr. Sharp traveled much, and he always brought me back a present of some kind. He would put the box or package on the bar. "This is for you, James," he would say, and walk away.

Fortunately Mr. Sharp was wealthy, for he seemed to enjoy being cheated out of his money by other men of his kind. He told me that he always started in the morning with ten thousand francs in his pocket, but that there were many times when he went home without anything. He often insisted on buying drinks for those present, not by setting them up all around, but by going from table to table like a waiter, or even a beggar, saying "*Voulez-vous un martini, monsieur?*"—Do you wish a martini, sir? The recipient of this favor might be a little surprised, not recognizing it as a kindly gesture. If he refused the martini, Mr. Sharp would usually order it for him anyway. Sometimes Mr. Sharp's generosity took turns that seemed fantastic to one who did not know him. But like so many men of this kind, Mr. Sharp could not stand any teasing or kidding, and upon occasion he would walk out, nose in air, insulted, though he might be back in half an hour completely recovered.

The fairies, particularly, have a hard life among the normal men, who often resent them, especially after a few drinks. I always watched for fights between two such groups—watched to protect the normal men, for the pansies were usually excellent fighters, despite their effeminate ways. There is a reason for this. Such a man knows, from boyhood, that he must defend himself against society, sometimes with his fists, and he often takes the precaution to study boxing with experts.

Then, too, these men almost seem to have an international organization to protect each other, to pay each other's bills, and to fight for their rights. The women do not stand together in this way, which proves that they have retained at least one of their feminine characteristics!

There were three kinds of such men: those who were conspicuous by choice, those who were obvious but tried to be inconspicuous, and those who hid their characters under a great pretense of being he-men. There were also the sex-adventurers who came to Montparnasse willing to try anything once, even homosexuality, in search of a new thrill. Women did this too, though less often than men.

My observation is that women of this kind are more jealous than their male counterparts, and that the latter are more true in their affections. The two seldom mix, though the men often have very fine friendships with normal women. In fact, a great affection often exists between one of these men and a quite normal woman who has no sex interest in him whatsoever. The fairy sometimes uses a normal woman to attract another man in whom he is interested. The women play this game too, though less often.

There are, too, those who pretend to be homosexuals yet are really quite normal. It is a little game. A man will give every semblance of effeminate qualities in order to reach the confidence of some women who would thus feel quite safe in his company. Then, at the appropriate moment, he will disclose his true character. Women do this too in order to reach certain men.

What I could never understand is the passion some normal men have for abnormal women. I have known several cases of this, in particular one involving an internationally known American newspaperman. I think he must have set a style, for since then it has become somewhat smart for a Don Juan to "collect" such specimens.

I once knew a man, a normal man, who fell in love with a beautiful girl in Montparnasse. She, too, was in love, and they were married after a short courtship. But unhappiness came at once, for they discovered that they were not as normal as they had thought themselves. They were very miserable.

Finally they worked out a solution by retiring to a small town in the country where they were unknown. He shaved off the beard he wore, donned women's clothes, and they settled down as two women living together. As he had very soft blond hair, it was easy for him to pass as a woman.

This arrangement went on for about six years, when I lost track of them, and the two were extremely happy!

THE EDUCATION
OF A BARMAN

Ernest Hemingway says the most interesting part of my life was before I went to Montparnasse, and so perhaps I'd better tell something about those events which culminated in my becoming a barman to the world's greatest haven of drinkers. Personally I did not find any great pleasure in those earlier years, but perhaps they were a sound schooling for my life in Paris.

It all began in the town of Rhyl in Wales in 1897. Rhyl was, and still is, a summer resort, with fine white beaches from which rugged mountains rise. It is a picturesque spot, I am told, though I myself have not been back since 1897.

In those days the summer colonies at seaside resorts were entertained by troupes of minstrel singers or pierrots, and it was to one of the latter groups that my father was attached. Twice a day he and his fellow actors amused the crowds on the sands, and in the evening they gave a performance at the Garden Hall.

One September evening my father was playing his act, which included some gymnastics as well as comedy, when my mother walked down the aisle of the theater holding me in her arms. When she neared the footlights, my father looked down just in time to see her throw me over the prompter's box onto the stage. With rare presence of mind, he jumped forward and caught me before I reached the floor.

"There," said my mother. "Take your Goddamn child!"

The audience, appreciating a good piece of comedy, applauded vigorously, and some even demanded an encore.

But for my mother and father it was no joke. She swept out of the theater in a fit of high jealousy, and neither my father nor I saw her again for many years. As for me, it was my first appearance before the public—age, three months. Actors rarely come much younger.

After my mother so dramatically broke up our family, Father was forced to send us children away, as he could not care for us himself. Daisy, my older sister, was sent to a convent school and I was given into the care of Father's sister, Mrs. Bedelia Carter, and her husband, who lived in a cul-de-sac in Salford, near Manchester.

My first memories are of that cul-de-sac, which was called Barlow's Croft, near Chapel Street. It was very narrow and very dirty, and we lived at the further end, in an old tumbledown cottage badly in need of repair. The cottage had a living room and kitchen downstairs, with a coal hole, and upstairs were two small bedrooms. My aunt and uncle had seven children of their own, so we were somewhat crowded, as you can imagine. The older children slept in one room while my aunt and uncle slept in the other with two or three of the youngest. But even in these small quarters, many cumbersome pieces of furniture had been crowded in.

My uncle was a hawker, and every day he pushed his cart through the streets of Manchester, selling vegetables, fruits, and flowers, from which he made a very modest living. Of course we had plenty of vegetables—all that were left over from the day's hawking! I learned to hate vegetables in those days, and as a result I eat far too much meat today. I have no doubt vegetables are good in moderation, but to see the same plate of potatoes and boiled cabbage day after day gives one a permanent disgust. Not only did I have to live on potatoes, I also had to peel them. As soon as I could hold a paring knife, that was my job. Each child had his job, and I have always thought I had the worst. If you have never pared potatoes for ten persons day after day, you cannot understand! We consumed five pounds of them at each meal!

In winter we were pretty cold sometimes, for that was the dull season in the hawking trade. When my aunt could afford a little coal, we had a fire in the living room, but there were many days when the house was filled with that damp Manchester chill and nothing to relieve it.

I suppose our life was only that of hundreds of other poor people. I'm glad it's over.

When I was seven I began to attend the St. John's Cathedral School in Salford, a dull place which I did not enjoy. Discipline was very strict and we lived under the daily threat of being sent to a reform school. We felt that once we were in a reform school we would spend the rest of our lives in prison. I never played truant from school because of this fear.

We were punished for our faults in the old-fashioned way, that is, with a cane. Five minutes lateness in the morning brought one stroke, and three strokes were administered for further lateness up to half an hour. For anything really serious we were severely beaten. I cannot remember a single instructor who made the slightest effort to teach me anything. Of course I was required to learn sums, and spelling by rote, but I always made the least effort possible, and determinedly forgot everything as soon as I could.

When school was over at 4:30 I had to go right home to peel potatoes, and sometimes run errands, too. My aunt never let us play in the street or with other children, for fear the neighbors would see how badly dressed we were. I don't know why my aunt was so pretentious, though she said it was because she "had seen better days." Of course our clothes were very ragged and she had little time for mending. On Sunday she would fix us up for church as best she could, with many pins and last-minute scrubbings, but the rest of the week we spent all our time indoors, except when an errand necessitated going out. If the law had not required it, I do not think she would have let us go to school.

Of course we did not work all the time. We had our games, indoors, and very often we were quite happy.

I forgot to mention that my aunt was very religious, and always attended early mass, to which we went, too. My uncle, who had been converted to Catholicism somewhat against his will, rebelled rather violently at times against all this churchgoing. And in particular he rebelled against giving part of their little money to the church. But my aunt always won him over. There was no resisting my aunt, and it wasn't because of her charm, either!

Finally my uncle was appointed to make the collections at church on Sundays, and that honor did much to soften him. However, he never became an enthusiast. His only real interest was in newspapers, which he bought in quantity for wrapping the vegetables and read aloud to my aunt every evening. I can see him now, standing near the window—he always stood—reading every item, column by column, while the children played, talked, and even screamed around him. It did not matter that these newspapers were often three or four weeks old; he pored over them as though they were just off the press.

Two or three times I decided to run away, to find another home where they had no potatoes, where I wouldn't have to go to school, but always, after walking all day, I returned to the cul-de-sac at night. There did not seem to be another home.

The bright spots of my young life were the weeks when my father took me away for vacations, which he did almost every summer. My father was making money, yet, acting on the out-of-sight-out-of-mind principle, he sent very little to my uncle and aunt for me. But when he took me on vacation he would exclaim at the poverty of my clothes and at once buy me fine new ones.

We always went to a seaside resort, where we lived in a boarding house that had what seemed to me the most marvelous food in the world. And there were many nice ladies who made a great fuss over me, from which I gather that my father must have been handsome and attractive. In the evenings I went to the theater with him, sitting in the "royal" box (which was seldom sold) and feeling very grand. He always dressed me in white sandals, shorts, a sweater, and a small Turkish fez. It makes me happy to think of those days.

Back in Salford I went on with my schooling until I was fifteen. The law required us to go only until we were fourteen, but my aunt made a mistake in my age, and so I had an extra year. I was pretty angry when I found out about it. As a matter of fact I found it out myself. One day it occurred to me to get a copy of my birth certificate, and I discovered that I had been born on the twenty-fourth of June, 1897. I also discovered that my name was Charters and not Carter.

While still attending school I had had several small jobs for Saturdays and Sundays. There was one which I took on quite voluntarily at first, but later greatly regretted. It happened that one bright spring morning during my Easter vacation, when my uncle was setting out for the produce market, I asked to go along, anxious, as always, to escape my aunt and the potato peeling. Rather to my surprise, my uncle consented and away we went.

My uncle found the arrangement greatly to his liking, and it was repeated as often as possible. I pushed the cart while he walked along crying his vegetables in a deep lusty voice. But first we would go to a big market to buy the vegetables. His specialty was potatoes, though he handled other things as well. While he did the buying, I stood guard beside the cart, for my uncle could not keep an eye upon it, being very shortsighted. Then we tramped through the streets of Manchester, from one end to the other, in all kinds of weather. When it rained I put a sack over my head, but never thought of wet feet or the cold. In a way this job was a blessing for me, for it made me very strong and hardy, and provided the background for my boxing career.

My first job after leaving school was for a man named John Heywoods, a wholesale book dealer; my next, for a dry-cleaning firm called "My Valet" with offices in the business district of Manchester. My task here was delivering and collecting clothes for businessmen in nearby buildings. I liked this work very much, for it kept me out-of-doors and always seeing something new. Sometimes I made deliveries in the suburbs, in which case my fare was paid on the tram. Often I walked both ways in order to save the money for myself. I still lived with my aunt and gave her all my pay, which was six or seven shillings a week, though she allowed me a few pennies for cakes, of which I was very fond. To see me now, no one would believe that in those days I was thin and scrawny, and always hungry.

When I grew a bit, the firm bought me a tricycle to facilitate deliveries. I loved riding on it, racing down the streets, through the traffic, helter-skelter.

The firm prospered during the year I was with them, so much so that they bought a delivery truck and I was discharged. I have always thought I contributed something to their success, and that they might have found a place for me, but I suppose all business-people are hard-hearted.

I had seen the shop of a very fashionable hatter's, named Pellet's, while working for the dry cleaners, and I decided to apply to the managers. I was accepted as a messenger, delivering new bowlers to members of the Exchange next door. I made a bit more money here, and often received handsome tips. After seven in the evening I made the deliveries to the suburbs and there were many days on end when I must have walked ten miles or more. People were very kind to me, the first sympathetic kindness that I had ever received, except during the short vacations with my father. I remember especially several young parlormaids in grand houses who made a fuss over me and even gave me handsome teas. This was, I think, my first consciousness of women. I can still remember one of those parlormaids with large blue eyes and black hair, very neat in her starched cap and collar and black dress.

And here, so early in my career, began a habit of which I have never been able to break myself. Try as I will, I can never seem to get anywhere on time. To me punctuality seems a petty, unim-portant thing. I am always willing to stay over to make up my lateness, but others look at it differently, I find. At Pellet's I was usually late—or even *always a little* late. I couldn't help it. They were quite satisfied with my work otherwise, I believe, but my lateness annoyed them. And so, after six months, they discharged me.

My aunt was more than ever determined that I should be apprenticed to a "good honest trade," as she called it, and so I started as beginner in a steel window-frame factory at three or four shillings a week. I liked this work.

Also, in a sudden rush of ambition, I decided to make up for my neglected schooling by attending a free night school. However, the ambition ran out at the end of two weeks and I never had another opportunity, a fact I have much regretted. Through the school I was able to join a boys' club, and this I continued to visit even after I had quit the school. I loved fighting and I took to boxing gloves like a duck to water. Being very small and having no technique, I was badly beaten at first, but this did not discourage me in the least. I liked fighting like nothing I had encountered before. I also joined the Boy Scouts and went on many fine hikes with them.

But I was having difficulties with my aunt, because I thought I was big enough to look after myself without her advice and help. She thought so too. And so one morning, after I had been fired from my last job, I was packed off, with all my things, to Liverpool, where my father lived with his new wife.

During the advancing years of our childhood my father had lost most of his interest in Daisy and myself, because, he said, we resembled our mother, whose memory was a torture to him. And so, when my aunt proposed that my father take me into his house, Father was distinctly opposed to the idea. "It will be too difficult, considering I have a new wife," he said. But the new wife, much to everyone's surprise, said she would be very glad to have me.

In Liverpool I went into another steel shop as an apprentice, but was finally discharged for my usual sin, being late!

Boxing now became a more absorbing interest with me than ever. I even began to think about making some money out of it, for one afternoon when I attended a sideshow at a circus, the manager, a big man with romantic mustaches and a long whip (as though we were animals!), asked for volunteers for a good scrap with the gloves. Shy as I was, I volunteered with another boy, and we went in like a couple of young tigers. In fact we fought so hard that the manager had to separate us and stop the fight. We were then allowed to pass the hat and took three shillings apiece in pennies.

From that time on I gave up cinemas and dances and devoted myself entirely to my gym club, where I received a hard training from professionals. It was really a club for professionals, and I was allowed in only because I showed such enthusiasm. As I gained experience, I was used as a sparring partner for some of England's best.

My first public fight was in the Liverpool stadium when Jimmy Wilde beat Johnny Rosner for the flyweight championship of the world. Another boy and I were among the preliminaries on the program. It was the first time I had been before an audience since I was three months old, and it made me nervous—so much so, in fact, that I could not take my eyes off the crowd, even when I was hit! The other boy was more used to the limelight and he took it naturally. Yet, despite my stage fright, we put up a good six rounds—the best event of the evening, they said later, for the main feature was a great disappointment. I lost our bout on points.

During the following year I fought in twenty-six preliminaries, always as a flyweight, of course. At first I was rather badly beaten, but I improved rapidly under the skilled hand of my manager, who knew a great deal about boxing. Most of the fights were in Liverpool, but we also took numerous trips to Manchester, and once or twice we fought in Blackfriars in London. I received two pounds if I won and thirty shillings if I lost. It was a small fortune to me, either way.

I grew considerably during this year, for I was now seventeen, close to being a skilled workman in the steel business, and a professional boxer who had appeared in London. I began to look forward to a career as a boxer.

After I was discharged from the steel shop I started to work for the London and Northwestern Railway, delivering parcels, and later became a railway messenger.

In the summer of 1914 Father took me to the seaside town of Prestatyn for my vacation and I remember very well the day war was declared. The news came while Father was in the middle of his act, and they whispered it to him from the wings. Father stopped the act and made a little speech to the audience, telling them we were going to have trouble, but that they must keep calm. Then he went on with the act.

From then on we saw soldiers every day on their way to France. I was excited about the war, and of course very anxious to join, but they wouldn't have me, first because of my age and second because of my lack of height.

When the government took over the control of the railways I became an apprentice in the switching yards. I liked switching because of the outdoor life and because of the danger. It was work that could not be relegated to women, and so the government decided to incorporate the workers into government service. Thus, despite my shortness, I found myself working for the army, if not actually enlisted. In fact, it was much better than enlistment in one way, for I earned two pounds a week. This, added to the money I earned from boxing, provided a very fine wage in those days. When I was eighteen I thought of joining the Bantam Regiment for service in France, but I liked the railway work, and I was told I was more valuable there, where I had had training, than I would be in the army, where I would have to be taught something new. I spent the entire war period in the railway yards, working very hard, for Liverpool was a big embarkation point for British soldiers and later for American troops.

It was here that I had my first contact with Americans, and I liked them very much—such fine, big men, always ready for a drink and a good time, or for a fight. They had a training camp at Nutty Ash, near Liverpool, and I spent some of my spare time out there, listening to their stories of America and helping them with English ways and manners.

I still lived with my stepmother. She was very fond of the theater and used to take me to all the musical comedies that came to town, especially when her own son was away at the Tiller school, learning singing and fancy dancing. I think I saw every musical comedy of that time.

One day, when I was still a boy, Father presented me to the famous Little Tich, who made a great impression on me. He was of extraordinary build, something less than human. He had five fingers on each hand besides the thumb, and six toes on each foot. The calves of his legs were in front, and on his face was the biggest and longest nose I have ever seen, Jimmy Durante notwithstanding. I was fascinated, and could not take my eyes off him. He was double-jointed in every joint, I believe, and a splendid acrobat. On the stage he did a comedy act, tap dancing, and he was also a very good singer. His first wife was English, tall as a lamppost, but he later divorced her and married a French woman. Years later I served him with champagne at Pigall's in Paris, but he did not recognize me, and I dared not speak to him.

All during the war I continued with my boxing, though opportunities for fights were not so numerous. Many times I gave exhibitions for the soldiers. Once, at Birkenhead, I was on the same program with Ethel Levey, the comedian, who sang "What a Beautiful Day for a Wedding in May," and also "Abie, Abie, My Boy, What Are You Waiting for Now?" She was a very good comedienne. Years later I served her, too, in Paris.

After the war I took a fancy to go into dining cars, and as a start I was offered a job as assistant waiter in the Railway Hotel in Liverpool, but at the last moment I went into the Midland Adelphi Hotel instead. This was an entirely new life, from switching freight cars to switching dinner plates, but I liked it. I liked it so much that I even neglected my boxing! I particularly liked wearing a frock coat and bow tie, in which I felt like Ford himself. I had never had work that I liked so much, I was wearing good clothes, seeing fine people, and learning to be really polite. I took to the work so quickly that in a month I was promoted to a position as full-fledged waiter.

This hotel was a very fine one, with a swimming pool, theater, coffee room, grill room, French restaurant, and a beautiful lounge. I was very happy in all this elegance which I had never seen before.

There were many Americans stopping at the hotel, some of whom were very kind to me and gave me big tips. I soon learned to act differently with them than with the English. The English people are very formal and polite, but the Americans are more friendly and natural, though both like quick and careful service.

Among the clients of this hotel were many of the important racing people—owners, jockeys, and trainers—and I came to know some of them. One Grand National week I was much excited over serving the great jockey Donoghue, with whom I struck up quite a little friendship.

At first I was in the coffee room, then in the grill room, and finally in the French restaurant. Here the headwaiters were nearly all Italians, who were surprised that I learned the business so quickly. They tried to help me, but said that to be a headwaiter I must know French. The easiest way, they said, was to go to France for a year and work in a hotel there. After a few months they arranged for an exchange of waiters with the Hotel Meurice in Paris, whereby I was to go to Paris and a French waiter was to come to Liverpool to learn English. And so in June 1921, I went to London, and from there to France.

I cannot well describe my first impressions of Paris. I was still a provincial boy from Manchester and Liverpool, and to be suddenly thrust into a foreign country, where I did not speak one word of the language, was a great shock and a wonder to me. Everything was so different! Paris was so full of life and animation, the cafés so gay, the temptations so many, the language so difficult! The first two weeks were like a dream, a sort of enchanted garden full of friendly people.

I made considerable effort to learn French and get ahead in my work. I liked Paris and determined to stay there, and I wanted to see all of it that I could. Well, I may not have visited all the museums, but I certainly have seen all the big hotels!

I was at the Meurice for several months. The King of Spain was staying there then and I saw him frequently, but he had his own people to serve him. Then I went to the Carlton. I needed a change, I thought, and experience in other departments of hotel work. At different times I have been dishwasher, waiter, assistant to the cook, in fact about everything one can be in a hotel except cook or owner. I am sure today I could go back to hotel work and make a good showing for myself.

From the Carlton I went to the Crillon, then to the Majestic, then to the Continental and several others. I never stopped more than a month in any place, for I was very restless and jobs were easy to get.

One day a fellow waiter told me about the sunshine on the Riviera, so I decided to go down there, for Paris was cold and damp in December. First I worked at the Hotel Masséna in Nice, as assistant to the barman. It was a new experience, being behind the bar, and I must admit I didn't understand much about it, but it was fun to see that row of faces in front of me and listen to the conversations—discreetly, of course, very discreetly.

After a month in Nice I went to Ciro's in Monte Carlo, and later to the Winter Palace in Menton. I found that bar work was even better than being a waiter.

When the season closed I returned to Paris and started on another tour of the big hotels, with the addition of cabarets and bars to the list this time. There was a little café and restaurant in the rue Boissy d'Anglas where the hotel men hung out when not employed. All the hotel managers knew about this café and would telephone there whenever new help was needed. I spent plenty of time sitting in that café, but I knew I was sure to get a job sooner or later.

My first job after returning from the Riviera was at Jack's Bar, later known as Johnny's, in the rue Port Mahon. The proprietor was Jack Saunders, and one day, after I had been there a month or two, the police came and took him away. I had not known what was going on, but Jack was convicted of selling dope and given nine months in prison, while his partner in the racket, a chemist named Green, was deported to England. It was then, I think, that I first heard about "rackets."

Chips (who was later at Harry's New York Bar) then became

manager of Jack's Bar; Frank was chief barman, and I was his assistant. I left after a few weeks because the hours were too long and the pay very small.

I next worked at the Bar de l'Opéra which was connected with the Café de la Paix, under Fred, who was half French and half English. He was an old-time barman who had worked in America before prohibition and also in England. I owe a lot to Fred, who was very kind and helpful to me. With great patience he taught me all he knew about the bar business, how to make cocktails and other drinks, and how to handle the clients.

I remember an amusing incident here when a client ordered a porto flip. I made it and said to the waiter in my best French, "Porto flip!" A while later the client asked me why I was so slow with his flip.

"What did you do with that porto flip?" I asked the waiter.

"Porto flip? I thought you said *porte au flic!*" ("Take it to the cop.") I looked out the window and saw the policeman in the square bending his knees and rubbing his hands in token of great enjoyment!

When the summer came again my restless spirit decided I needed sea bathing, so I put in a season at the Hotel Royal Palace in Ostend and later worked for a short time in Brussels.

And now some thirst for adventure made me want to go farther afield. During the summer at Ostend I had taken a great fancy to the sea. Going from port to port seemed better than moving from bar to bar, so I decided to go to sea. Although I had lived for years in Liverpool, this desire had never come to me before.

Well, why not? I went to Antwerp, expecting to walk aboard the first boat as waiter or barman. But things were not so easy in the sailoring business. Antwerp was full of old salts who had had years of experience, and few of them were able to find berths. I had no friends and little money. At the end of a week I was broke and forced to go to the British consul, who had heard the same story so many times he was sick of it! He offered me a ticket to England, but I did not want to return home. He then suggested the Salvation Army. I stayed with the uplifted sinners for more than two weeks.

The army people were really very kind to me, gave me food and a decent place to sleep. Of course I had to go to church and sing hymns to pay for it, but that was easy work.

In the meantime I had written to George Wright, headwaiter at the Meurice, asking for enough money to get me back to Paris, and this he sent me as soon as he could.

Once again I was back at the café in the rue Boissy d'Anglas, playing cards with the boys and waiting for a new job. In those days they called me *l'Anglaise-Qui-Bouffe-Pour-Dix* (The-Englishman-Who-Eats-For-Ten) because I used to finish my own meal and most of what the others left too. I was making up for all those years in Manchester. Even so, I was still quite thin.

I soon found work, sometimes as an assistant barman and sometimes as a waiter, though I had lost my taste for waiting on tables. Very often I took temporary jobs for a few days at a time, for I was still restless and also I wanted varied experience. At one time or another I must have worked at every big café and nightclub in Montmartre, including Pigall's, l'Abbaye de Thélème, Le Royal, le Perroquet—where I often served Mistinguett—Le Caveau Caucasien, Zelli's, and a Russian place called the Yar.

In the end I found a job that satisfied me at the Hole-in-the-Wall on the Boulevard des Capucines. Pedro was the barman and I was his assistant. But things did not work out as well as I had hoped. The main difficulty was Pedro, who catered almost entirely to the French clients and was very casual with the English and Americans. I soon saw that it would be easy to fill up a bar with English-speaking people if the barman went about it in the right way. I saw, too, that the latter spent far more money than the French. But Pedro could not understand.

Nevertheless I had a few English and American clients of my own, particularly the late John O'Brien, American newspaperman, who came in almost every day.

It was in this bar that I first developed any personal friends among my clients, or felt any personal regard for them. The Hole-in-the-Wall was an alternate drinking stop to the New York

Bar around the corner, and we used to get many of their clients from time to time.

I remember particularly Charlie McCarthy, who was an old, old man and had spent many years in Paris. It was he who founded Luna Park in Paris and other amusement parks in different cities in both Europe and America. He promoted the Jack Johnson–Frank Moran fight in Paris in 1914, on which the receipts were considerable. However, Charlie suspected that he was to be cheated out of his fair share, and forthwith tied up all the money so that no one could touch it—including Charlie himself—without a general settlement. Moran and Johnson never agreed to Charlie's terms, so the money stayed in the bank, accumulating interest, until his death. In his latter years Charlie had almost no money, yet he stubbornly refused to compromise with the fighters. If he had, he would have still had a very comfortable income for the remainder of his life. Charlie died in 1925.

Michael Arlen was an occasional visitor to the Hole-in-the-Wall, and I can see him now, with his dark complexion and hair and his fashion-plate clothes, leaning against the end of the bar. He was not a very sociable person, as I remember. Later I saw him at the Dingo, the Parnasse, and the Falstaff in Montparnasse, always with a crowd of admirers around him and he usually trying to escape them.

Another client here was Mrs. Nell Henry, wife of the jockey Milton Henry who founded the New York Bar in 1911. Mrs. Nell, as she was often called, sold it just before the war, but repurchased it in 1920 when it was going very poorly . Mrs. Nell was a colorful character in the best traditions of New York City, having been a godchild of old Tom Foley, Tammany chief.

A person I knew slightly in those days and admired much was Frank Meier, the celebrated barman of the Ritz and formerly of the Hoffman House in New York. Frank, who is still at the Ritz, is one of the masters of tact in the profession, and he can handle his crowd in both the men's bar and the women's side (or steam room, as it is called) at the same time, without ever losing his poise.

One day the agent for Bacardi rum told me there was a job open in Montparnasse at a bar called Le Dingo. He said it was a bar for English and Americans.

I had never worked in Montparnasse before, for it seemed a bit off the beaten track, but I liked the idea of working with my own people. Lou Wilson, the proprietor, hired me as assistant barman and waiter as soon as I applied, and that was the beginning of my many years as bartender to the Quarter.

THE BARS OF MONTPARNASSE

I have worked in most of the smaller bars of Montparnasse at one time or another and each has had a character different from any other. Often the difference was one of atmosphere or it was caused by the attitude of the owner.

After I left the Dingo I joined Old Man Dingo in a new venture in Montmartre called the Imperial. Many of the Dingo clients followed me up there, and it was then that I first realized what a following a barman can have.

The Imperial was very successful, due particularly to the good music. Mostly we had American college orchestras, one from Yale, another from Harvard, and another from Penn State. Frisco introduced the Charleston to Paris at this bar.

But I fell ill about this time and left after only six weeks as barman. It was too bad, because I had a good job and got on well with Old Man Dingo. Later, after a rest, I returned to the Imperial as headwaiter, for a month.

Yet Montmartre was not Montparnasse! I quit the Imperial at my first chance to return to the Left Bank, and became a barman at Pirelli's, later called the College Inn.

Pirelli was an Italian, as you might suppose, with a very pretty wife, two children who were then eighteen months and three years old, respectively, and a nurse. He installed them all in the bar, which was one of the smallest in Montparnasse! The pretty wife he made cashier, which was a good idea, as people don't mind paying money to a good-looking woman. He himself was manager, and the nurse and the children he parked behind the bar, where I stumbled over them every time I turned around. To add to my worries, the baby often cried lustily, driving most of the clients out of the bar for the evening. I really don't know how I survived eight months at that place. Fortunately the baby didn't cry all the time, and we did have many good parties there.

Pirelli was not very popular with the clients, largely because he insisted on washing his hands in invisible soap all the time. Pat Guthrie used to say that he would wear his hands out altogether if he continued rubbing them so much. Also he had an annoying habit of slapping on the back (hard!) anyone he thought was a good client. Pirelli never knew how close he came to being beaten up on many an occasion.

Very familiar figures around Montparnasse in those days were Laurence Vail, his wife, the former Peggy Guggenheim, and his sister Clotilde Vail. They were having dinner in Pirelli's one night with some friends, while at the further end of the room were five Frenchmen, chatting and laughing. Vail, who was sometimes taken with sudden tempers, decided the Frenchmen were making fun of him and his guests. Coming to the bar, he picked up a bottle of vermouth and a bottle of Amer-Picon and threw them in rapid succession at the five at the back of the room. One man just missed being killed by a fraction of an inch, and the dent in the wall could still be seen at the College Inn the last time I was in Paris!

Of course there was a riot at once. The Frenchmen landed on Vail, and when the police arrived, they landed on him too. He was finally taken to the station in a wheelbarrow. He was tried, and succeeded in escaping prison sentence only with great difficulty.

But out of all this came a romantic event. The Frenchman who was almost killed struck up a great friendship with Vail while waiting for the case to be tried. Through this friendship he became much interested in Clotilde, Vail's sister, and they were married shortly afterward. I attended the wedding, and Clotilde told me I was the best-dressed man there because I had on a frock coat and striped trousers. It is something to be the best-dressed man among such wealthy people!

The Vails were noted for their large and exciting parties, at which I was nearly always barman. It is fun to be barman at a private party and give people all the drinks they want without thought of payment or credit, though it entails much more work for me. It was amusing, too, to watch the people who drink only beer or other cheap aperitifs at a public bar, for they usually make a dive for the whisky and champagne at a private party.

Later Peggy and Laurence were divorced, and Vail married Kay Boyle, the writer.

In the end I had a fight with Pirelli because he was rude one night to Pat Guthrie, Lady Duff Twysden, and Louise Coons. They had been good clients of mine and I had to stand up for them. I walked out with them and never returned.

After that I took the bar at the Parnasse, across the street from the Dingo. At that time it had just opened under the management of Fred, who looked like an English butler and was a former headwaiter at one of the big boulevard cafés. He was a Swiss with decided pro-French sympathies.

His idea of making a successful bar was to fill it up with girls who would attract the men. I have never found this a good system, for the only men who spend money because there are girls present are drunks, and a bar full of drunks is a hard crowd to handle. However, Fred found the drunks to pay for the girls, and everything was successful. In fact, the girls would get clients by taking them away from the Jockey and the Dingo, especially for the downstairs room where we had an orchestra and dancing.

The Parnasse stayed open all night, and most of its clients, who were largely French, came after the other places closed. After my arrival, however, the place began to fill up with English and Americans, and soon it was a madhouse in which one could rarely find a seat, and never a table, during drinking hours. The receipts jumped from five hundred francs to three thousand francs a day.

But I had made a very bad deal for myself. In the first place I was working under Fred and he controlled all the money. I took in from two hundred to four hundred francs a day in tips, but he "allowed" me only thirty or forty, keeping the rest for himself. And in the second place, the architect of the building had played me a dirty trick! When he had designed the place the year before he had forgotten to put in a kitchen. No one had noticed at the time, though the place was designed as a restaurant! So a pantry with a stove was rigged up in a small room, but all the dishes had to be washed at the bar, the only place with running water. I washed them, for there was no one else to do it. So what with a roomful of heavy drinkers and the dirty dishes, I never stopped working for hours at a time. Many and many a time I have worked fifteen or sixteen hours at a stretch!

The Parnasse was a very drunken place, and that's why so many nationalities managed to get along without killing each other. Fred handled the crowds pretty well, too, despite his very definite favoritism toward the French. Fred was really quite a character, a man of sixty with wonderful vitality. But he would often fall asleep from sheer exhaustion, either sitting or standing. His favorite remark was, "What would you like to drink? A steak and potatoes? Something hot?"

But, even with the best precautions, fights in the Parnasse were a common occurrence. Once a Spaniard made personal remarks to Jopie Wilson and Kay Musgrave, whereupon Muzzy hit him in the face and the battle was on. I rushed in, knocked the Spaniard out, and then found myself fighting a crowd of them. With the help of Fred I fought my way out. The Spaniards left then, with much screaming and hollering.

Another time a crowd of South Americans began fighting with a group of North Americans and I had to carry the former out, one at a time.

I really did not like the Parnasse very much, and I lost a number of my faithful clients, who did not like it either. Of course, these fights and other disturbances did not happen every night, or the police would have closed us up. Whole weeks would go by without any serious incident. This was fortunate, because I had many fine clients who would not have returned had the bar been too tough.

I left the Parnasse after a few months to help open a place in the rue Boissy d'Anglas called Chez Mr. Finney, owned by Charlie Clopp, a graduate of one of the big American universities. He hoped to make the place a rendezvous for visitors and students, and for a while it went very well; but as soon as the summer season was over, business fell off and I returned to the Parnasse, this time with a better financial arrangement.

This was the year when the American Legion held its convention in Paris, a convention which was a great disappointment to most of the bartenders. Elaborate preparations had been made to entertain the Legionnaires, not only in the bars, but even in police jails especially furnished for drunks. No one seems to have remembered that nine years had elapsed since the war, and that in those nine years the former members of the American army had grown up a bit, that they had perhaps married and settled down, and that their wives had learned to make them behave. When Paris saw this crowd of middle-aged men with their families, prepared to visit the Louvre and Napoleon's Tomb rather than Montmartre and the Folies Bergère, there was much sorrow and disappointment.

A sculptor with a commercial mind produced for the occasion a statuette of an American soldier dancing with a woman whose only garment was a French flag which completely covered her. The statuettes sold like hotcakes, not only to the Legionnaires, but also to others. However, the French government thought that a woman clad only in a French flag was indecent. It caused a great scandal and ended in several persons being deported.

My next bar was the Trois et As, which I have described in another chapter. After I left there I joined with Henri, the former manager of the Jockey, who had just bought the Monaco, a bar of the same sort, which he renamed the Jungle. The Jungle was a noisy madhouse filled with a young crowd of the rah-rah type. The Jockey had been interesting, but the Jungle was puerile.

And yet we made money hand over fist. Henri must have made a small fortune, I should think, for we served inferior drinks at fancy prices on the excuse that we had an orchestra. Most of my regular clients would not drink the Jungle liquor and did not come there often.

But Henri, who had formerly been a secretary in the French

diplomatic service, had a talent for attracting a crowd. He would get such stars as Kiki, Marcelle, Chiffon, and Vivienne to entertain, and for the orchestra he had Paire, Brooks Cowing, Donny Duncan, and Sasha, a Russian saxophonist. These names were enough to fill the place every night, and I made more money than I had previously.

Then I had an offer to open as barman at the Falstaff, a new bar with fine decorations. It seemed just my type of place, where my personal clients would be well satisified. So I left the Jungle with considerable regret for the good money I had been earning. I was glad, though, that I did go to the Falstaff, for that became a big success after a while.

I said the Trois et As was my best bar because it was the most exciting, for something was always happening there; but from the strictly bartender point of view, the Falstaff certainly takes first place. I have always regretted that I left.

The fine part of the Falstaff was the atmosphere, which was both gay and churchlike at the same time. The Old English form of decoration, the wooden-paneled walls, had a calming effect upon the heavy drinkers, restraining them from too much noise or disorder that might annoy others; yet it was a cheerful place where people enjoyed themselves and liked to sit about. It was neither formal nor entirely informal, but struck the happy medium.

And right here let me present a man who was known variously as Joe the Interpreter, Joe the Sailor, Joe the Cook, and Joe the Barman. He was my assistant at the Falstaff, and a good pair we made at that time, for I liked Joe and we worked together smoothly.

Joe was Dutch, of German extraction, and as a boy in Holland had learned the baking trade. For some years he sailed the seas as chief baker on various vessels. Then for a long time he lived in Havre.

When I first knew Joe he had been working around Montmartre and Montparnasse for some time and had built for himself a small following. People liked Joe for his rather brusque manner, for the deep scar on his face, for his slang, and for the way he talked out of the corner of his mouth. Women, especially, found him attractive, and he was, for a while, by way of becoming the local Don Juan.

Joe loved to imitate a strong Oxford accent when English people were around. In ordering beer he would say, "James! Three pints of draughts, please!" or he would ask, "James, have you had your tea? I've had mine." Newcomers would be much puzzled by such conversations.

It was about this time that I entered a cocktail contest at the Apollo Theater and won a handsome prize, thanks in part to Jane Marnac, the French actress. I had not known her previously, but when she tasted my cocktail she took a great fancy to it and immediately brought all her friends to taste it, including some of the judges. I received a handsome cocktail shaker with my name engraved on the front, and felt very proud.

Ever since I had been in Montparnasse people had asked me from time to time why I did not save my money and open a bar of my own. They encouraged me to believe that I could make far more money. Finally I decided to make the break. Across the street from the Falstaff was a little nightclub called the Bec de Gaz, the "Gas Jet," which I was able to rent. I did not have enough money to pay the guaranty of twenty thousand francs, so I took as partner a man named Eddie Ruffi, an old-time Swiss bartender whom I knew but slightly. He had formerly been barman at Ciro's in Deauville and Monte Carlo and should have had a certain clientele. He borrowed ten thousand francs from Roger, the barman of the Crillon, and I had saved enough to pay the other half.

I had known, of course, that the Bec de Gaz did not cater to English or Americans, but had I realized the true character of the place at the time, I would have hesitated to take it over. My first job—and it was a hard one—was to get rid of the old clientele, composed of Arabs, butchers on a spree, and many shady characters from the tough district behind Montparnasse. The butchers I remember particularly, for they often came in their butcher aprons all covered with blood, asking for the *poupées*! Well, the "dolls" were there all right, and they had to be got rid of, too, if I was to make this bar agreeable for the clients I had always catered to.

I succeeded in this after a few months, and the place was filled every night with the people I had formerly served at the Falstaff, though never in such numbers. The atmosphere of the bar was not as pleasing as that of the Falstaff, and I was somewhat disappointed with the result of my change, but nevertheless I hoped in time to have it redecorated and slowly build up a good business.

And then came something I had not foreseen. No one had told me that a world economic crisis was to begin in 1929! When it came, many Americans, panic-stricken, rushed off home, leaving the bars of Montparnasse in a sad way from which they never recovered.

Even so, I suppose, we could have struggled along, making enough to pay the rent and living decently, had not Eddie turned out as he did. I do not know what happened to Eddie, for he was a nice chap and I had every confidence in him. At first we worked very well together. I handled the bar and drew the crowd, while he acted as floor manager and took charge of the ordering, paying of bills, banking, etc. But Eddie had a wife who did the cooking, and, in between times, made jealous scenes. That was the first difficulty. The clients didn't like to hear her screaming at him from the kitchen.

Then Eddie took it into his head to be jealous of me, and when I was not there, often said that I had left the place, implying that it was a good riddance. I can't understand Eddie's motive in this, except that he was very proud of being a barman himself, and that he had begun to drink quite a bit. He was never drunk, but always managed to keep a good edge on, night and day. In any case this jealousy of his lost us a lot of business, as I discovered later.

Eddie became careless about the bills, too. At first he paid them regularly, but then he began to fall behind. It was not because there was no money to pay them, either, but he was salting it away, I suppose, or perhaps he spent it. One day he did not show up, and I have never seen or heard of him since. I was left without a sou and with bills amounting to thousands of francs! I had been what you Americans call a boob!

Of course I had to give the place up. There was nothing else to do. All my friends were broke, and I could not raise enough money to pay all those bills. The landlord and the liquor companies were very decent about the thing and more or less let me off, though if I ever have sufficient money I will pay those bills yet. It is the only time in my life I have ever owed money I didn't pay.

It was at the Bec de Gaz that I first met Lionel Leslie, formerly of the British army, and a cousin of Pat Guthrie. He came in after I had been there for a month or two and had finally succeeded in getting rid of the old clientele of the bar. When he appeared in workman's clothes, a cap pulled over his face, I thought, "Here's another I must ease out some way." However, he looked tough, so I decided to be polite to start with.

"*Que voulez-vous, monsieur?*" I said. ("What do you wish?")

"*Un demi blonde*" ("a mug of beer"), he replied. I then told him the price, thinking that might discourage him, but it didn't. He then proceeded to pull from his pocket a copy of the *Daily Mail* and spread it out on the bar. The Countess Eileen, who was sitting at the bar, said to him in French, "You can't read that! Where did you get it, anyway?"

"At a paper shop," he replied in English. Even then it was some time before I was convinced that he was an Englishman.

The Bec was the scene of one fight that almost ended in a serious tragedy. A young couple had been quarreling after numerous drinks, and, although I had done everything I could to quiet them, the man, at least, would not be soothed. Finally he raised a chair and brought it down squarely on her head! I was really very frightened when I saw it coming down, but she was saved by a miracle. Her head went through the rungs untouched, while her shoulders were only slightly bruised!

One of my faithful clients when he was in Paris was Augustus John, the English painter, for whom I always kept on hand a bottle of good Calvados, of which he was very fond. The first time I saw this husky man with his long, light beard I hardly knew what to make of him, but we soon became friends, as he was a very sociable person with a simple, companionable nature.

When I was at the Bec, John brought in his son Robin, of whom he was very proud. The son had trained to be a boxer and Augustus John had hoped he would continue, but the boy gave it up in favor of painting.

There was quite a group of artists who came to the Bec, all of them close friends. Horace Cole, who is famous for his sense of humor, was one; also Jacob Epstein, the American sculptor who stayed away from his native land for twenty-five years. He was usually accompanied by his two Indian models, who were quite beautiful. Rowley Smart, the British painter, was another of this group. Rowley was one of the old-timers of the Quarter, and it was there, in Moret, and in Giverny that he painted most of his pictures.

John Storrs, the sculptor, often came in, in those days, too. He had just inherited a large fortune, but one of the conditions of the will was that he spend eight months of the year in Chicago. "Have you ever lived in Chicago, Jimmie? It's worse than Manchester!" he would say.

Other good friends who followed me to the Bec were Tommy Leaman, who always called me Yumping Yimminy, and the artist Oscar Fabresse, who made many cartoons and sketches of me. Once when I was at the Falstaff I had been on an auto trip with Bill Walsh and we had had a breakdown on the way back. Unable to get to the job on time, I had wired the proprietor. Fabresse pasted the telegram on a piece of cardboard, and around it made a sketch of me walking along with a toy horse one of whose wheels was missing.

Fabresse published an entire volume of sketches of me entitled *La Vie Fantaisiste d'un Barman de Montparnasse* (The Strange Life of a Barman in Montparnasse).

After the collapse of all my hopes at the Bec de Gaz, I went to the Strix, though by that time it was no longer a Swedish restaurant but had fallen into Italian hands and the name had been changed to Romano's. In the early days, before it was the Strix, it had been a French restaurant in which Modigliani had paid for his meals by decorating the entire surface of the walls. After Modigliani's death, when the value of his paintings suddenly jumped from nothing to high figures, the walls with the paintings were removed for sale to collectors.

Romano's was, for me, rather a gamble because I did not think the place would go. Nevertheless I went about filling it in my usual way. It always seemed to work. Starting with an empty bar, I went out and found ten or twenty personalities whom I knew fairly well. As soon as I had these in the bar the place was made, for dozens of others would follow them. I offered no inducement to get a bar going, but a few weeks later I gave a free party to which everyone was invited.

I have found that a bright, cheery atmosphere is the most important thing in a bar. Decorations should be simple and are secondary. As long as there is food on hand, its variety is of little importance to the bar. Prices should be fairly high in order to make the place exclusive. The American free-lunch idea is a good one, but Europeans do not understand the system and refuse to learn it. It sounds expensive to them.

Romano's bar had a pleasing atmosphere, and the place went overnight. I was delighted to see it filled with the sort of crowd that I had had at the Falstaff.

I got a big crowd into Romano's one of the first nights by a trick, in which Rowley Smart, who was always ready for such things, went to the Dôme and told everyone in sight that there had been a suicide in Romano's. You should have seen them come running! People I had never seen before or since, others who for some reason never come to my bars, all flocked in to see the suicide! A newspaperman even had his paper on the phone, waiting for the details! Nearly everyone who came bought at least one drink.

But it is a steady crowd that counts in a bar, regular patrons who come back year after year. I always managed to keep the nucleus of such a crowd, but when people began to desert Montparnasse, my clients thinned out in proportion.

"MY LIFE AND LOVES"

For a person who has seen so much of other people's love affairs and seems to talk so glibly about them, I have been singularly stupid about my own. I guess I don't really know much about women. I should have learned from the experiences of others, but I didn't.

My first passion was for a little Burgundy girl, assistant cook in the Dingo, by the name of Jeanne. She almost got me into a peck of trouble and I can't remember her with much pleasure.

Jeanne had a *croix de vache* on her forehead, which should have warned me, but it didn't. I was even a little proud at having such an experienced woman! The *croix de vache* is a cross cut on the face with a knife by a man to whom the woman has done wrong. It is a trick of branding of which the apaches are very fond, and her last amour had left her this cross to remember him by.

But he must have regretted her nevertheless, because one day he appeared at the Dingo and called her out. There on the sidewalk he pulled a gun and told her to be prepared to come with him, that he would be waiting at the subway when she was through work. He was an Arab with a dangerous face.

"I have six bullets," he said, "five for you and one for myself." I suppose that was real apache love, but I didn't appreciate it. One can't fight bullets, so I took her to the police and they posted men at both the Vavin subway station where she got on and at the St. Paul station where she got off. But he must have suspected something, for he never appeared, rather to my disappointment.

After that dramatic beginning I made her leave her work and set her up in a small hotel apartment. But she was young and she was tough, and that's a bad combination. She was one of seven sisters, to whom she introduced me, and they were all just as tough, though some of them were not so young.

I really thought she was pretty grand and I felt very much in love. I gave her clothes, I gave her money, and all evening long, when I was working, she had nothing to do. That is, she had nothing to do with me. Later I found that she took my money to buy drinks for her tough sisters and the tough sisters' boyfriends! That meant I was keeping at least thirteen persons supplied with liquor, and I could never be sure it wasn't fourteen.

The Arab, whom she called Toto, also was around, but he always escaped me. The police had given me permission to beat him up on sight, but I never got the chance. Once, after a quarrel, Jeanne took a job as waitress in a restaurant on the Boulevard St. Michel, and I had reason to believe that she was meeting Toto somewhere in the neighborhood. On one of my nights off I had been celebrating with two Italian waiters, and late in the evening, after we had consumed eleven bottles of Asti Spumanti and were feeling decidedly "warm," I decided to find Toto. He had become an idée fixe, so the three of us started to scour the Boulevard St. Michel. I had on me a revolver which I had bought when I first came in contact with Jeanne.

Well, we didn't find Toto, fortunately, and the Italians finally persuaded me to return to the Dôme, where Brooks Cowing did me a good turn by relieving me of the revolver without my knowing it.

The next morning the thought of what I might have done with that gun frightened me. I sold the gun and I saw Jeanne but once again, to tell her everything was finished. I have never seen her since.

My next love was a Bretonne named Germaine, a girl of a better family, who was a lady's maid in a big house. I was at the Parnasse Bar at this time, and she used to see me there, leaving with me when I was through. She already had a baby, whom I supported as long as I knew her. We had good times, Germaine and I, but it didn't last long. One week she did not appear at the Parnasse, and a few days later a letter announced that she had departed "for some place far away." Several months later I received another letter from her, bearing an address in the Old Port of Marseille, asking me if I would take her back. I never replied.

And now comes the grand passion which made of me an even bigger sap than I had been previously. It happened this way.

Jim, a friend of mine, and I had been on a spree one night. About noon the next day we found ourselves, with a strong thirst for coffee, in Les Mousquetaires, a café on the Avenue du Maine. The place was crowded with shopgirls in the noisy chatter of their midday meal. Near us sat two whose looks were striking, to say the least. One, on whom I had my eye, was indeed a handsome girl, resembling Pola Negri of the movies. I fell for her headlong before we had exchanged a single word. We looked at the girls and they looked at us; they smiled and we smiled. So Jim wrote a note in French asking them to meet us at the same place the following day. The handsome one, seeing the note, came over and took it without a word.

The next day they were there all right, and we became acquainted at once. I was very much excited and on my best behavior, for they were fine-looking girls.

The following Sunday the four of us went to St. Germain-en-Laye for the day and a gay time. It was part of the Fourteenth of July holiday, and everyone was very lively. After four or five aperitifs in a little bistro in St. Germain we thought we owned the town! We hired an old fashioned *fiacre* nearby while we joined the crowd. The old *cocher* was having just as good a time as we were, I think, for I know we bought him a great many drinks. We finally settled down in one place because the *cocher* took a shine to the proprietress and would not leave. We left him there, finally, still dancing with her.

I was working at the Falstaff at that time, and was due to work that night. Reluctantly we returned to Paris, had dinner, and settled the girls in a café across the street from the Falstaff. They were to wait for us until the bar closed and then the party was to continue. I could not leave the bar, but Jim ran back and forth across the street twenty times or more during the evening. When the bar closed we joined the girls and continued the party until well after dawn.

The Pola Negri girl was called Madeleine. She was nineteen years old, and lovely. I wanted to marry her, and suggested it within the first few days after I had met her. She liked me, too, I thought—she must have liked me a *little*. She said she couldn't marry yet, that her family would not let her until she was twenty-one. Two years seemed like a long time, but I was willing to stick it out.

"I will introduce you to my mother," she said, "and you can arrange things with her." But I never met her mother, for she kept putting it off. Maybe she did not have a mother—I never knew! At first she said she lived with her mother, but later she told me her mother was going away and she was going to live alone. By this time she had changed jobs and was working at the Louvre department store.

So I rented an apartment for her, furnished it, provided her with money, clothes, and elaborate presents. I even took her to Deauville for an expensive three weeks' vacation. During the two and a half years I knew her I spent more than a hundred thousand francs on her, and all the time we lived as pure a life as two children. We were children, I guess, or at least I was one.

Then one day I saw her on the street with another man, a tall gigolo type, and of course I was jealous and suspicious. I accused her, but she said he was an old friend, and I relented. Yet I was still suspicious. There were little signs. She was going out all the time I was working, for instance. Being a barman is certainly hard on one's love life! We work in the evening when everyone else is playing, yet we can't lock our girls up. Many of us wish we could! And also we can't have them in the bar, because the owners won't stand for it. It's tough.

Finally Madeleine and I had a real quarrel, and I wrote her breaking off everything. But when she got my letter she came to me at once, cried, pleaded, and said she was doing nothing wrong. I relented, but my suspicions weren't gone entirely, so I decided to find out once and for all.

I knew a girl who worked in a lingerie shop in Montparnasse, whose name was Margot. She was leaving her employer and he had advertised for a new shop assistant. So Margot procured the job for Madeleine, who was delighted not to have to go so far to her work. It was a better job anyway.

But the new job for Madeleine was part of a conspiracy between Margot and myself, for during the two or three weeks while Madeleine was learning the business, Margot was to find out if Madeleine really intended to marry me or not. All too easily Margot found out that Madeleine had no intention of ever becoming Mrs. Jimmie Charters—and never had had, what's more! I was furious, bitter, and disgusted. We had a row right in the shop that must have shaken the walls. She had even admitted to Margot that she had a lover who lived near the Étoile! What a sucker I was, and what a ride she gave me! It makes me bitter to think about it even now.

Well, I thought I was cured, especially of French girls. I was down on the whole race. But—well, you know how it is! Some months later I was introduced to Marylene, who was someone new in my experience—a girl who wouldn't let a man spend all his money on her! Today she and I are married and very happy.

THE END OF MONTPARNASSE

Montparnasse really ended in 1929 with the beginning of the depression in America, but as an artist colony it had been on the wane for some time before that. When the sightseers, visiting firemen, and tourists descended on the Quarter in ever-increasing numbers the artists and writers began to move out. Most of these tourists were Americans drawn there by articles in the home press on the wildness of the Left Bank. Then came the crash, and most of these new customers were forced to return home, leaving behind only a few diehards who literally could not tear themselves away from the scene of past glories. Then, during the next five years, even most of them were forced to move. Some returned home, some went to Majorca, where the cost of living was lower, and others retired to small provincial towns for the same reason, coming up to Paris only once a year or so.

All this caused the bar business to dwindle to practically nothing. Today, I am told, only the Coupole is filled every night, and even there an Anglo-Saxon is a rarity. I myself continued on for a while at Romano's, then at Frank's until it closed from lack of business. Finally, after a summer on the Riviera and a short stop at Suzy's Bar in Paris, I returned to London, where life has been pretty gay these last few years, though it will never compare to Montparnasse in its heyday.

It is interesting to reconstruct the old days in Montparnasse because it was a period that will certainly go down in the history of art and literature. But it is perhaps even more interesting because so many thousands of people from all over the world found self-expression of one kind or another and a general release from

KIKI

from a drawing by Hilaire Hiler

inhibitions—the greatest wild-oat field the world has ever known! For most of these their months or years on the Left Bank mark the highlights of their lives. Such a combination of circumstances as produced Montparnasse is never repeated in the same manner.

Several years ago, when I first thought of writing this book, I turned to Laurence Vail for advice, and with his permission I will quote parts of a letter he wrote me at that time. It might be called the swan song of Montparnasse.

My dear Jimmie,

One hears all over Montparnasse these days (and any day) that Montparnasse is dead, *passé,* no more. Growls liverish old-timer: "Where are the deep artist-drinkers of 1923?" Grunts old-timer with hangover: "Where is the bona fide bohemian who starved on absinthe and midinettes for the sake of pure art?" These laments are in part justified. The Quarter sniffs less of wet corduroy and turpentine, more of carbon monoxide, Quelques Fleurs, near gin (gout américain). It's gone Pittsburgh and Ternes, Berlin-Montmartre for the *petit bourgeois* purse. In a way, too, it has suffered the fate of Imperial Rome. Overrun by the barbarians: happy German families in ulsters, hardy Scandinavian raw-fish eaters, trans-Mississippi school teachers. And, too, many pretty little girls and boys from Yale, Oxford, Bryn Mawr. It's not their youth I object to, more pink than *doré.* Why will they look so healthy, so clean and nice?

But most depressing, to my mind, is the French invasion. Oh, I grant a few natives are necessary for service and atmosphere. Who could replace the old sullen *garçon* who stares through you or the other way when you order a drink? There should be a sprinkling of prostitutes with grudges, sleek ancient *violeteras,* a couple of Frenchmen with sketchbooks and beards; and the Madonna of the Lavabos should be a type. A *petit Parisien* carrying a large canvas across the boulevard also improves the picture. Not with these is my quarrel, but with hoi polloi of papas and mamas, *tantes*

Juliettes, *cousins* Alfreds, *petits* Roberts who sit for hours over two bocks, one quart Vichy, and three grenadines. A morose contrast to the days when, in less than two hours, Flossie Martin and other notables could pile towers of saucers half a meter high.

Times have changed, my dear Jimmie. And this reminds me of an old souse who staggered into the Dôme one midnight. This was long before your day; Greenwich Village had not taken over the Quarter yet, and the Dôme was a rendezvous of a number of Russians who later achieved a certain temporary notoriety—Trotsky, Gorki, and Co. Well, the sight of these sober politicians got the old tippler's goat. So this was an art colony! No *joie de vivre* anywhere! Ah, the 1860s! Those were the days!

I gathered presently that this ancient toss-pot had once been a *chef d'école* of a group of artists so revolutionary that they called Rimbaud a "*sale bourgeois*" and Verlaine a "*vache à papa*". This clique lived in the country, in the lofts of some farms that were later destroyed to make room for the Lion de Belfort. Every Friday, he and a few cronies, old farmer-artists, would ride to the capital. They would tether their horses to a lone oak that stood then on the very spot where the subway station Vavin now hourly disgorges several hundred French families debating whether or not they can afford a whole glass of beer. Then, going down a dark lane, now the rue Bréa, they would enter a sort of cabin, Montparnasse's first cabaret—it was called the Sélect. There they met their muses and models, all members of the aristocracy, who had managed, as women do, to give their husbands in the Faubourg Saint Germain the slip. Women of extraordinary daring, according to the old souse. Often they would leap on the tables and dance in their petticoats, revealing bare knees and sometimes a fringe of a drawer! All were emancipated. Not one that ever put water in her *vin rouge*! And there were several that smoked pipes and spat!

"Ah, those were the great days," said the old drunk. "We never went home before half-past ten! Night after night I saw the moon rise!"

Thus, for every old-timer, the wild days are ten, twenty years ago. Where is the old billiard table of the old Dôme? You should have seen Kiki in her first coats of paint. Still, the man of forty will return to the scene of his youngster drinking bouts. I do. Frequently. The first hour in Paris and I am hopefully searching the terraces for a drinking companion, a boon Pernod pal. Alack, forty million Frenchmen and not one face I know. Still it's six P.M.; time Flossie Martin came down to breakfast on potatoes and gin. And no sign of other early drinkers: Bob Coates, Iris Tree, Bob McAlmon, Tommy Earp, Mary Reynolds, Ossip Zadkine, Hiler, *père et fils,* Lady Duff Twysden, Renato Borgati, Nina Hamnet, Jacques Baron, Roger Vitrac, Kathleen Cannell, Walter Shaw, Harold Loeb, Alfred Kreymbourg, Countess Monici, Foujita, Mina Loy, Kiki Allen, Kiki, Dotto Taylor, Louise Varese, Florence Gilliam, Ernie Hemingway, Pierre de Massot, Nancy Cunard, Slavinsky, Jane Heap, and Eugene MacCown, all of whom did their bits—and what bits—to put Montparnasse on the map. Then suddenly, as I decide to cross the river forever, I see a face I have seen God knows where among faces I knew. He, too, seems to recollect that somewhere at some time he has seen my face. I go over to him, hail him as a long-lost friend. Then, as I survey the multitude of French beer drinkers sitting smug and thrifty along the boulevard from L'avenue to Dôme: "What's come over Paris?" I say. "There's no one here."

"There are a few people in Paris," replies the face I successfully avoided talking to and looking at from 1910 to 1933, "you will find everyone at Jimmie's. He's opened a new bar in the rue————."

And this happens, my dear Jimmie, each time I return to the capital. Anyone that is left of "everyone" is to be found at your bar. If McAlmon isn't at the Falstaff, then he's just left to spend two weeks in Minorca, making a few contacts and writing two or three books. If Hemingway's not at Pirelli's, that means he's not in Paris; he has been called to the afternoon funeral of a matador.

Oh, there are some old faces we will never see again. There are the traitors to the cause of good drinking and gay living who have gone in heavily for a "career." But those don't count, Jimmie. They will never ripen into wise owls, mellow bums. It seems X is a successful portrait painter in London (for fear of a libel action I won't mention his name), and Y is a family man, and Z is a wealthy advertiser in Sioux Falls. Traitors all, and cowards. Small fry, my dear Jimmie. In truth, human beings can be roughly divided into two classes. There's the fellow who drinks and yarns at Jimmie's from cocktail till dawn. Then there's that other individual, that nobody, the man in the street.

My dear Jimmie, I cannot in the blue years and brandies remember at which of your bars this and that memorable incident took place. Was it at Pirelli's that Tristan Tzara, prince of *Dadas,* and Allan Ross MacDougal, traveler and newspaper reader, fought with soft bare fists till one had convinced himself that he had dealt his opponent a black eye? Another unforgettable contest, Kisling versus McAlmon, was also staged on your premises. I also remember a gray November morning when you yourself, no dilettante at fisticuffs, floored giant Homer Bevans[1] for having dared to mutter a naughty word in the presence and direction of the American Undset, the Irish Colette—Miss Djuna Barnes. But such brawls were exceptions; your smooth drinks and tact made rather for happy conviviality than for fighting drunks and *vins tristes.*

The arts also flourished in your varoius barrooms. It was in your place near the Panthéon[2] that Hemingway narrated his first bull and fish stories to the blond elf of Vassar—Edna Millay. The Surrealists, Aragon and Breton, evolved their theories at the Falstaff over your port. Nor were musicians and painters of note wanting in your cosy and vivacious *estaminet.* Many times have I known Antheil and Varese, Kisling, Derain and Van Dongen to seek inspiration and exhilaration in your artful long drinks.

As you changed premises every year or so, your barroom was always a novelty, *le dernier cri de Paris.* It is the little bar near the Panthéon that I remember best. Tommy Earp lived at Foyot's then. So did Mary Butts, Mary Beerbohm, Maitland, Bodson, Iris Tree,

---

[1] No, Mr. Vail, it was not Homer.

[2] Trois et As bar.

so it was easy for them to drop in for a dozen whiskies and sodas from nine to three. Eileen Lane dwelt around the corner and she always came in for dinner, drinks, supper, drinks, and breakfast with Brancusi, Man Ray, and Radiguet. The celebrated Carmen supplied fireworks, Aleister Crowley his magic, and Ezra Pound and Ford Madox Ford were frequently present to contribute the intellectual note. But the pace was too swift for them. So one became the sage of Rapallo, the other the prophet of Toulon.

What a book it will be, Jimmie, if you put everything in! For yours has been the privilege to see *Tout Paris* in their cups. Not only *Tout Paris,* but *Tout Londres, Tout Berlin, Tout New York.*

Good luck to you, and all my wishes for a grand success.

LAURENCE VAIL

THE BOOK MUST END

The selections that follow have been taken from the English edition of *This Must Be the Place*, published in 1934. When the American edition was being prepared for publication three years later, the editor Clifton Fadiman excised these and other passages. The title "The Book Must End" is the final chapter in the English edition, and since several of the passages below come from that chapter, it seemed appropriate to use that title for the concluding part of this new edition of the book. [H.F.]

MY FIRST VISIT TO MONTPARNASSE

At first I stayed with English friends at night, and worked as a helper at the Meurice during the day. The work was light and I had considerable time to amuse myself with my friends. Ideal June weather, too, encouraged me to have a gay time. It was the second day, I think, that I was introduced to Pernod, which is a substitute for absinthe. I liked Pernod. It didn't seem strong and it was very pleasant to the taste. In England I had led a very abstemious life, never drinking and never smoking in order to keep in training for the ring. But now I smoked and drank frequently. Drinking is in the air in Paris, especially in spring.

Two weeks after my arrival I was walking down the Rue St. Honoré at 11:30 in the evening with three or four friends of mine. I admit to having been a bit stewed, the first time I had ever been drunk in my life.

"Come on, Jimmie," one lad said, "you're a fighter; we want to see you hit someone." I looked around for an opponent, but we were apparently alone. However, standing in front of me was a fire-alarm box—about my height too—and in an instant I hit it with all my force.

What possessed me I don't know, except that I was drunk. The door of the box flew open and let forth a terrific din, waking echoes and *concierges* all along the street. The other boys, scared by the noise, urged me to run, but I couldn't move. They left me standing there looking at the alarm box in amazement.

Soon the *pompiers* arrived in a big wagon with hose and ladder. The chief fired questions at me, while the thirty-odd firemen ran around looking for the fire. I replied in English that I had hit the box by mistake, and they finally understood me, especially when a *concierge* or two said that a band of drunks had done it. My friends were gone. The *pompiers* were decidedly annoyed. And so they started to take pokes at me with their fists. I tried to fight back, but it was a bit hard against thirty.

Finally the chief made them stop, and he handed me over to two bicycle police, who took me to the *poste,* or police station. No one spoke English, and I guess I was too drunk to make a case for myself, anyway.

The police kept me in a small room overnight, a room that was very hot and stuffy, and they would not give me any water. They took my tie, my shoelaces and belt, to keep me from escaping, I guess. It seemed a funny way, but I had had no previous experience of police stations. I was very miserable after I began to sober up. I slept some, but I was so thirsty I waked every few minutes.

In the morning I was taken to the office of the Commissaire de Police, which was in another building. I walked between two policemen with my hands in my pockets, as they instructed me. At the Commissaire's office I waited six hours while they sent for George Wright, the headwaiter at the Meurice, to interpret for me. Everything was carefully explained to the Commissaire, who made no comment. The headwaiter pleaded for me that it had all been an accident, that I had been drunk, but still the Commissaire said nothing. I said good-bye to the headwaiter and was taken back to the cell in which I had passed the night.

I was beginning to feel pretty desperate by this time. I had visions of spending days in that same room, always without water and precious little food.

That evening, though, a big black wagon came for me, and I was driven across the city to the famous prison on the Ile de la Cité called the Conciergerie. At that time I did not know the history of that prison, how thousands and thousands of innocent persons had been killed there, or I would have been scared to death.

About a year ago a friend suggested that we go there to see the cell once occupied by Marie Antoinette, but I couldn't do it. I was afraid it might turn out to be the one I had occupied, and when the guards saw me again they might keep me.

I spent two days in the Conciergerie, in solitary confinement, with plenty of time to sober up and think what a fool I had been. Of course, I was indignant too. It seemed silly to go to all this fuss over what was really a schoolboy prank.

From the Conciergerie they took me to the big Prison de la Santé, near Montparnasse. It was my first visit to Montparnasse.

I began to wonder if the city of Paris was taking me on a sight-seeing trip of the local prisons. I was told nothing; I was not allowed to communicate with my friends except in French, and of course I could speak no French, much less write it; I was simply put in a cell and left there to rot, for all I knew.

Have you ever been in prison for more than overnight? It is something you can read about all your life and never appreciate until you have experienced it. I don't wonder that they say prisons make the criminals worse instead of better. There is something about a prison that makes one feel so terribly lost and lonely.

The French had a great sense of humor when they named this prison *la Santé,* which means *health.* The health it brought me was an attack of indigestion and ulcers of the throat!

I was put in a cell with two other prisoners who were waiting trial on murder charges. One had killed his wife, and the other had killed his baby. They were fine men and very kind to me. The wife-killer spoke a few words of English, for his wife had been one-quarter Scottish, he said, and he had lived for a short time in Edinburgh.

There was one table and one chair in the cell, and each had a mattress and a blanket on the floor. Rather a change from the Meurice! We were waked at six in the morning and ordered to go to sleep at six in the evening. In the morning we cleaned our cell with a brush, taking turns day by day; we were given ten minutes' exercise in the large stone courtyard, and we spent the rest of the day pacing up and down the cell like caged lions in a zoo. The two killers had some consolation in being able to talk. The wife-murderer was being held while they tried to find his accomplice, and if they did not he hoped the evidence against him would be so weak that he would be freed.

Our food in this palace of health consisted of dishwater soup in which floated a few starchy beans, and hunks of hard, dry bread. The bread was so tough that I broke a tooth on it the third day. Also I developed ulcers of the throat. When I asked the guard to take me to the prison doctor he only laughed, or threatened me with physical punishment.

One thing I was able to do in the cell, however, was considerable shadow boxing, as long as the guard, who passed every half hour, did not see me.

At the end of ten days I had begun to think that I would pass the rest of my life in that cell. In fact, I was making great efforts to learn French so that I could pass my declining years with the comfort of a little conversation. And then two guards came for me and marched me away. They're not going to let me die here in peace, I thought; they're going to take me on another tour of the prisons! And then I remembered that prisoners waiting for the guillotine were always held at the Santé. Perhaps they would guillotine me! You get funny notions when you're in prison. You come to believe that anything might happen, and most of the time you wish it would, if only to relieve the boredom.

They didn't guillotine me, as you may have suspected. They took me across the city again to an examining magistrate, who, with the aid of an interpreter, brought out my long, sad story. The magistrate had a twinkle in his eye, and I got on famously with him, but when it was over they took me back to the Santé just the same.

Three days later, however, I was freed. A prison official handed me a paper, by which I later discovered that I had not been held for turning in a false alarm, but because I did not have a *carte d'identité*! As I was released without trial there is no police record against me. Now it seems like a huge joke, but it wasn't then.

When I was arrested I had £20 on me in English money, but no francs at all. They returned my money, and in addition gave me a few francs with which to get home.

Once released, I hurried away from the prison before they could change their minds about me. I did not know where I was, but walked in any direction until I found myself in front of a café called le Dôme, on the Boulevard du Montparnasse. I guess it was fate!

But I didn't stop for sightseeing. During the two weeks or more that I had been in prison I had not shaved, and now a straggling beard covered my face. I went to a barber's shop nearby and had it removed, paying with the francs the prison officials had given me. I then took a taxi to the Meurice, where the waiters and cooks crowded around me to hear my adventures. They thought it was a great joke, and after a while I thought so too.

THE INHABITANTS OF MONTPARNASSE

After years as a bartender, Jimmy made some perceptive observations on the people he served and on the impact that Montparnasse often had upon them. [H.F.]

There were always four kinds in the Montparnasse bars: the tourists who represented about a quarter of the clientele, the students a possible ten percent, the artists, writers and newspapermen about forty percent, and the remaining one-fourth the regulars, the hangers-on, the disillusioned (mainly as a result of love complications) and the habitual drunks. The latter often made of the bar an unhappy place, for each was possessed by a sadness he wished to recount to someone else.

The tourists and the students were looked upon with some suspicion by the others, but the bohemians and the disillusioned were usually fast friends. They appreciated each other, though the drunks often led the bohemians astray.

I think there must have been very few real bohemians in Montparnasse, that is, people of fine creative and imaginative powers, who live only for their work of today and care nothing for the future, who have no desire to build anything except a particular painting, statue, or book. But there were many who played at being bohemians, and even succeeded for a short time.

A free life for a year or so is a fine education to many smug young English and Americans who come to Montparnasse, *if* they go home before it gets the best of them. But it is sad to see those who can never get away from bohemia, for whom "art" is simply license, or others for whom it is an escape from life, a refuge from fear and cowardice. Some of these come, in the end, to trade on their reputations as bohemians, getting money from the bourgeois tourists or feeding their egos on self-importance and cheap glory.

I think I succeeded in Montparnasse because I had a warm spot for the bohemians and those who were trying to escape from their educations for a short time. One must not be too commercially minded to deal with these people; one must be sympathetic. It is very easy to be a bartender to dukes and princes. All they require is that you keep your place. But in Montparnasse I had to be the shoulder on which most of my clients wept now and then, and the repository of their confidences.

THE OLD CROWD

As Jimmy approached the end of his memoirs, he realized, as all memorialists must, that he had left unmentioned many of the characters he had known in Montparnasse. Into the final pages of his book he crowded as many of his old friends as he could remember, and extended apologies to those whom he would inadvertently forget. [H.F.]

I have written my allotted space in this book, and now that it is finished I feel as though I had barely scratched the surface. I have known hundreds in Montparnasse and about each one are a dozen stories. Many that I find I have not mentioned are celebrated in the world, though that means little to me; others are old-timers who should have a line, characters of Montparnasse.

When I arrived in Montparnasse in 1924 I was taken to the Jockey almost at once, where I started a long friendship with Hiler. I also met many of the people who later became my most faithful clients.

One of the most interesting characters of those days was Charley Ashley, who had led a remarkable life as a hobo in the United States. Just recently he wrote a book telling of these experiences. He has traveled from one end of the States to the other, "riding the rods," begging food here and there, doing as little work as possible. Finally he became a labor leader, a member of the IWW, and later a representative of the Soviet government.

As a bar companion Charley was very interesting, for he would tell many thrilling stories of his adventures, or he would sing hobo songs, such as "You'll Get Your Pie in the Sky By and By." He was also an excellent imitator.

Ashley had spent the war period in a cell in Fort Leavenworth, and after his release he went to Russia to join the new government. Later they sent him to England as the head of the Russian press service. When a Montparnassian, who had known Ashley as a sort of king of the hoboes, visited him in London he was amazed to see him surrounded by secretaries and flunkeys, and in luxurious offices. However, when this same Montparnassian later visited him, he was confronted by a detective.

"Mr. Ashley," the Scotland Yard man said, "met with an accident, I think. I believe he is in the hospital, sir." The fact is that he had been royally beaten up and was finally located in a police cell.

Link Gillespie, the journalist, was one who wanted to start a bar with me, an urge that moved so many of my clients. Link and I used to have long conversations, in which he invented most of the words on his side, I think. They were long, medical-sounding words and I am sure they could not have been real. They were rather a hindrance to the conversation, but we kept it up, anyway.

One day Link came into the bar around four in the afternoon. "I must have food and liquor," he said.

Thinking he was joking, I said that it was absolutely impossible. Link then went into the back room and wept like a child, because I had refused to serve him!

A person I much admired was Eddie Lanham. He had an adventurous career, having run away from home at sixteen or seventeen, worked his way around the world as a sailor, and ended, as they all do, in Montparnasse. Lanham wrote a book that I have heard much admired, called *Sailors Don't Care,* in which the sentimentality about seamen is exploited. Lanham comes from a very distinguished family, his grandfather having been governor of Texas.

Another writer of that time was Harrison Dowd, the poet, who was himself the main character in one of Bob McAlmon's books called *Distinguished Air.*

Two more writers who were great friends were Buffy Glassco and Graham Taylor, both Canadians and fine chaps. They would sit at one end of the bar, their little Scotty between them, discussing serious subjects that I did not understand and being superior to most of the others at the bar.

A client who has been to most of my bars is Fulton "The" Grant, as he is called, one of the great "womanizers" of Montparnasse. A great friend of his is Alex Small, who writes a column for the *Chicago Tribune*. Alex is a man I admire, for he seems very intelligent and learned, and I like to listen to him. One night Alex and I stayed out all night, while he talked and I listened. At nine in the morning we went to Fulton's with a package of chops and kidneys, woke him up to cook them, and then started the party all over again.

Rockwell Kent, the illustrator, wrote a book called N by E, describing a trip in a sailing vessel to Greenland, which ended in shipwreck. Kent was accompanied by two men, one of them June Cary. After the wreck June came to Paris in the corduroy trousers, much the worse for wear, in which he had made the trip, claiming he had no money to buy others. When they split down the back he held them together with safety pins and, thus costumed, took the boat for America. June had spent some time in Paris on a previous trip and was well-known to Montparnasse. His father is Lucian Cary, the writer.

While at Romano's I met an international figure in the world news at that time, Harry Gerguson, alias Prince Michael Romanoff, famed for his ability to impress the social climbers and extract money from them. When Mike, as he was called, came to Montparnasse everyone knew that he was no prince, as the papers had been full of him for several weeks before that. Anyway, Montparnasse is the last place to be impressed with titles.

But Montparnasse did like Mike very much, because he is a charming person, because he carries everything off with an air that many of the bohemians would like to imitate, and because many of us felt genuinely sorry for him. Especially after he left a French jail for the last time, and just before his return to America, he was a hero.

It is the opinion of many who know Mike that he is incapable of reform in the usual way. Mike is not a person who has had a hard time and turned to petty graft in desperation. Not at all. He has some kind of obsession that is beyond his own control.

It was three or four days after I first met Mike that he asked me to cash an American Express check for a hundred dollars for him.

"This is a perfectly good check," he said, "will you cash it for me?"

"Certainly I would," I said, "but I haven't got that much money in the bar right now."

"Well," he said, "take it anyway. Keep a couple of hundred francs for yourself, and give me the balance tomorrow."

Now this check belonged to an American woman who had taken a great interest in him. She knew his record perfectly well, she had no illusions as to his relationship with the Russian royal family, but she liked him and thought he deserved help.

And so she had paid his bills, had given him money, had started negotiations to get him a League of Nations passport, planned to support him for at least six months until he obtained it or found something to do. She entertained him in a style that should have suited his taste. In other words, he had everything to gain by playing the game with her.

Mike had had many opportunities of taking money from this lady, but only checks interested him. He took one from her checkbook, imitated the countersignature, and gave it to me. Unless the lady should not notice the loss of the check, he was almost sure to be detected, as only he and one other person, above suspicion, had had access to the book. When his baggage was searched tracings of the lady's signature were found and a blank check on her bank in America.

But the lady was still kindhearted and did not report the theft to the police. Instead, she reported him for failure to obey the deportation notice he had been given. On this charge he was given a month in a French jail. On his release he again appeared in Montparnasse, and I saw him at Frank's, a rather pathetic figure, for it was cold and he had no overcoat nor any money. Several of my clients offered to help him, but mostly he refused their aid with a peculiar show of pride.

Among my clients here were Bill Seabrook and Marjorie Worthington, the writers, who flew to Timbuktu for material for a new book. Seabrook, in his corduroy suit, is an impressive figure, and he was quite lionized for a while. He came from the best traditions of Greenwich Village, where he was connected with a restaurant on Waverly Place.

Another old-timer in bohemian life is Arthur Griggs, who is one of the very hard workers of Montparnasse. Two of the most liked were Sam and Charlotte Weller. Sam, who has seen much service in the air force, started the Necessary Luxuries Company in Paris, after the war, to supply fresh milk and cream to the hotels. With almost no capital he built it into a prosperous firm. Unfortunately both have been ill for the last two years, and this so preyed on Charlotte's mind that she committed suicide recently in New York.

Ena Mitchell was also well liked during her stay in the Quarter, particularly for her caustic Scotch wit. Jim and Ruth Clark were personages of Romano's too. His imitation of a YMCA worker is one of the best things of its kind I have ever heard.

John Russell, the Canadian painter, frequented the bar, too, often giving elaborate parties for his friends. Bill Buhler is said to be the first American to come to Montparnasse, forty years ago. Bill is well liked, with his chubby, humorous face, and his gift for reciting poetry.

Bill Butler, the Englishman who sells English language newspapers in front of the Dôme, is a familiar character too. He is an upholsterer by trade, but jobs have been hard to find in that line for a long time. He came to France during the war and never returned to England.

Pop Eaton came to Paris shortly after the war and has been struggling along between painting and photography as best he can ever since. Pop's good cheer never leaves him, and even when he is having the hardest times he is always around the Quarter with a pleasant word for everyone. Pop is sixty-five these days, and getting on, though he seems to have an excellent constitution. Lawton Parker did much to help Pop and recently Charlie Ogle came to his assistance when the landlord was about to put Pop on the street.

R. Howell Cresswell is another who has seen the Quarter in all its stages. For years he was Paris correspondent of an American magazine, living in the same hotel and never leaving Montparnasse. Cress, in a modest way, has probably done more to help the poor artists here than any other person and he deserves a lot of credit. He has also been a very good client of the bars, making the rounds almost every night, though he drinks nothing but beer, and not much of that. Cress always sits in the back of the room where he can view the crowd, never letting others buy his drinks, for he does not believe in creating obligations of that kind. "*Un demi-blonde au fond de la salle!*" is a phrase that always denotes his presence.

Cress has had two passions since he came to Montparnasse: the tomcat, Toto, that formerly inhabited the Dôme terrace, and Flossie Martin. Cress greatly admired Flossie and would sit happily for hours in any bar where she might be, content to watch her from a distance. It was a sad day for Cress when Flossie returned to America.

In recent years Cress has become greatly interested in spiritualism and will tell you amazing stories of séances in his room, if you ask him. This year Cress inherited 30,000 dollars and is leaving Montparnasse.

Edgar Adams, an Irishman who has become a naturalized Frenchman, is well-known in the Quarter for being more French than the French. Adams has been connected with the London *Times* in Paris for thirty-five years, much of which he has lived in Montparnasse. He knew Modigliani and others of the Quarter in its heyday.

But I cannot end this book without mentioning such well-known figures of Montparnasse as La Croix, an ex-boxer in the heavyweight class, and his American wife; Berenice Abbott, the photographer, who was a great friend of Gwen Le Gallienne; Floyd Gibbons, the war correspondent, known to many as the Purple Cow; Hank Wales, who managed the Paris edition of the *Chicago Tribune;* Walter Durante, who now represents the *New York Times* in Moscow; Otto Gaensslen, one of the oldest Americans in the Quarter; Jack Pickford, the young brandy drinker who finally did himself in; Charles Beadle, who is a white-winer and an old-timer too; popular Harry Crosby, who died so tragically; Jimmy and Elise Cosset, who ran the College Inn; little George Seldes, out on the trail of "stories that can't be told"; and quiet Mr. Dubois, painter and art critic.

Others I remember of those days are Robert Collier Washburn, who wrote the "Life of Lydia Pinkham"; Lorry Hammond, now married to the Princess Kropatkin, whose articles on Russia are well-known; Arthur Moss, who has just written an excellent book on Murger; Donald White, Raymond Gutherie, and Bill Godell, all former members of the Lafayette Escadrille; Stella Steyn, the Jewess with a broad Irish accent; Dudley Murphy, who made the films "Frankie and Johnnie" and "Black and Tan Fantasy"; Kitty Cannell, the short-story writer, now married to the French playwright, Roger Vitrac; Ruth Reeves, who has made a big business of her fabric designs in New York, and her husband, Donald Baker, who has turned inventor; Shorty Shoedsack, six-foot-seven creator of the wild animal films like "Chang"; Shorty Weigandt, who is now a cemetery guardian; and Slim Day, who is in the diplomatic service.

Others were Peter Powel, the photographer, who lost his American citizenship during the war because he fought in the French army, but later regained it; Captain Smith, who went from London to Italy in a canoe; the woman who was ashamed because she had a decided mustache on her lip, though when she had it removed she became a beauty; Sam Dashiel, an American journalist, and Hilda, his very English, ex-Tiller-girl wife; Captain Bunny Christiansen, who, though his legs are paralyzed, was a great success with the ladies; Bea Mathieu, who represents the fashion column of the *New Yorker* in Paris; Rea Brown and Flo McCardle, friends of Bea's, and also in the fashion game; Countess de Vitali, a great friend of Pat and Duff; Edward Titus, the husband of Helena Rubinstein, who published *This Quarter*; Louis Coons, a writer from Kentucky; Nels Jorgensen, the dashing Don Juan and breaker of feminine hearts, who got himself into a peck of trouble when he finally married one of his admirers; Jack Thomas, who always wanted what he couldn't have; Harold Loeb, who prides himself on his bridge and boxing; Steve Green and Sophie Victor, who have abandoned painting in favor of making movies; and Walter Shaw, the most credited man of Montparnasse.

But there have been so many characters of Montparnasse that I could go on for pages remembering people who left their impression on the Quarter. How can I leave out Peggy Marquis, Jack Pickering, Olivier Regnault, Mary Coles, Jo Davidson, Abe Honigsberg, Bourdelle, Julian Levy, Jerry Kelley, Steve Robinson or George Waller Parker? It would take too long to sort them out by years and associations. What is a book on Montparnasse without mentioning Arthur O'Neil, or Judy Bolegard, or Hunt Diederich? And where are Bob Woodlaw and Helen, Arthur Franck, Erik Satie, Lillian McCarthy, and George Biddle?

I know so many stories of the people I met in Montparnasse. I wish I could write an uncensored book. It would be lots more fun. And now I think of it, I haven't mentioned some of the old bistros that we went to after the bars closed: like the old Cicogne before it became fancy, the Rendezvous des Chauffeurs near the Gare Montparnasse, and the Falaise around the corner; also the Escargot on the Rue de la Gaité. Many nights they have been crowded until dawn or after, or at least until the Dôme reopened.

I hope that I have hurt no one's feelings in this book. I have been called the father confessor of Montparnasse, and I hope I have been appropriately discreet. When the news first leaked out that I was writing my memoirs, several survivors of the old days endeavored by threats or cajolements to make me promise that I would not mention them in any scandalous manner. Some of the Quarterites were really scared! I had to laugh. I never intended to make a book of scandal. In any case it would take twenty volumes to tell all the scandal I have learned in ten years in Montparnasse, and no publisher would print them anyway.

INDEX